On the Mythology and Triads of the

Ancient Bards of Britain

with Poems Lyrical and Pastoral

by

Iolo Morganwg (Edward Williams) B.B.D.

With his own notes

(Compiled by DEDWYDD JONES)

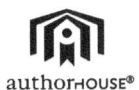

authorHOUSE®

AuthorHouse™ UK Ltd.
500 Avebury Boulevard
Central Milton Keynes, MK9 2BE
www.authorhouse.co.uk
Phone: 08001974150

First published by AuthorHouse 8/19/2008

ISBN: 978-1-4389-0829-8 (sc)

Printed in the United States of America
Bloomington, Indiana

This book is printed on acid-free paper.

published 1794
first proclaimed on Primrose Hill, Hampstead, London

These little collections are in loving memory of my father Major Francis Jones, Wales Herald Extraordinary.

I am greatly indebted to *Iolo Morganwg*, by Prys Morgan in the *Writers of Wales* series, University of Wales Press.

‘

TABLE OF CONTENTS

All of the above contents, from the 'Poems' to the 'Bardic Institutions, Triads, Notes, etc' are contained in the single volume, entitled, 'Poems, Lyrical and Pastoral' (1792.) Apart from a few brief interjections by Dedwydd Jones and Jonathan Harris, all the words are those of the great Iolo Morganwg.

Preface to 'Poems Lyrical and Pastoral'
by Iolo Morganwg:

'My little publications appears after a pretty long delay. Some obstacles occurred from the nature of my situation: these were unavoidable, but mostly unforeseen; others were thrown in my way by the mean machinations of Envy, that appears to have been at the success and valuable friendships that, for a while, I met with at opening of my subscription.

I had unfortunately, rather foolishly, reposed confidence in some that I once thought my friends; they became thus possessed of the knowledge how and where to injure me – and they did – let them enjoy it!

I had, and still have, an intention of going to America, partly to fly from the numerous injuries I have received from the boasted laws of this land, that are not, whatever one called Reeves, or his brother, 'Bearmonger', of Holborn Hill, may say, made equally for the poor as for the rich; and hardly an instance can be produced, where a poor man, unbacked by wealthy friends, ever obtained justice in our law Courts. Another motive is to ascertain the truth of an opinion, prevalent in Wales, on good authority, that there are still existing, in the interior part of the American Continent, the remains of a Welsh Colony that went over there in the twelfth century under the conduct of Madoc, son of Owen Gwynedd, Prince of Wales. Some frivolous anecdote-hunter inserted an account of my intention in one of the Bath papers, whence it was copied, in most of the London and many of the Country papers, with an intention that surprised me, on so trifling a subject. My enemies made a very good handle of this for the dagger that was now drawn against me: a report was, whisperingly, circulated, that my poems were not at the Press; that I was going (some said I was gone) to America, with my subscribers' money in my pocket. It was long before I heard anything of this rumour, which acquired some colour from my work not appearing at the time that I promised it; for, I was as ignorant of the nature of my undertaking, and of the printing business as anyone can well be. I was dilatory from other causes also; I was far from home and my family where all my little portion of happiness was centered; I was also conscious of the numerous defects and crudities of my pieces, which made me frequently linger over them before I would put them to the press, whilst a dejection thus occasioned disqualified me from making some amendments that I saw so requisite. There were gentlemen of the first abilities that would have assisted me, but I could not think of accepting their very kind offers; for, I was from the beginning determined not to put the least imposition on the public, but to give them the real unsophisticated productions of the self-tutored Journeyman Mason: under such a mental depression, I am convinced, that I have sometimes rather injured than improved my pieces. Some may not admit these things as an apology but they were occasioned by sensibilities that I am not ashamed of; and will not blame me.

About November 1792, I had printed my poems as far half the second volume, my little flock of cash failed, and I had not the courage to mention this to my printer, who, from what I have since experienced, would have been my friend, on this occasion. I informed my friends (why do I call them so?) of this: they had, unsolicited, promised assistance to me, if necessary, had even urged me to apply for it without any scruple; but all was silence; subscriptions that in some places, had been collected for me were with-held; I did not yet see the cause. I wrote an account of these things to Mrs and Miss Harriet Bowdler, of Bath; and these most amiably benevolent Ladies, to whom I had before been under a thousand obligations of the first magnitude, supplied me with what I wanted as soon as the profit could bring it. I am on similar occasions under the same obligations to my excellent friends in London Mr Owen Jones, and Mr William Owen. These Ladies and Gentlemen will dispense with those common-place phrases that express hypocrisy rather than gratitude.

Everything would have been very well now, and my poems would soon have appeared; but for, what I had always dreaded, on account of the deaths of one of my dear children, a favourite little girl, with whom went more by far of the joys of my life than can ever be recovered in this world – I went home immediately, and there, for eight or nine months, I remained. I forgive everything to my enemies but their having been the means of detaining me from home when my pretty little infant was in the hour of death calling upon me. There are a few, and they are of the most valuable part of mankind, to whom this circumstance will be no bad apology for the additional year of delay: I would not have been thus querulous , but that an apology was due to my subscribers; and what could be but the truth.

To those numerous Ladies and Gentlemen, by whom I have been patronized, I am, and shall be through life, gratefully thankful; and I trust that none will be offended at me for printing the names of my most distinguished friends in italics. Their number was too great to be otherwise thanked in this place.

Some of my best friend have urged me to give some anecdotes of my life. I have little of anything to say worth notice on this occasion. I was so very unhealthy a child (and have continued so) that it was thought useless to put me to school where my three brothers were kept for many years. I learned the alphabet before I can well remember, by seeing my father inscribe gravestones. My mother, whose maiden name was Mathews, was the daughter of a gentleman who had wasted a pretty fortune; she had been well-educated ; she taught me to read in a volume of 'Songs', intitled the Vocal Miscellany; for I could not be prevailed upon to be taught from any other book. My Mother sang agreeably , and I understood that she learned her songs from this book, which made me very desirous of learning it. This I did in a very short time, and hence. I doubt not, my original turn for poetry. There is no truth in that old adage 'Poetry is born, not made', for, I will venture to say, that a Poetical and every other Genius is made by some accident in early life, making an indelible impression on the tender mind of infancy.

I could buy no books; there was not at this time a single bookseller, except itinerants, that sold Welsh books in all Wales. the whole of my (or rather my Mother's) little library consisted of the Bible, some of Pope's works, Steele's Miscellany, Milton's Poetical Works, volumes of the Spectator, Tatler and Guardian. The Whole Duty of Man, Browne's Religio Medici, and a translation of Ovid's Metamorphosis, in the black letter, which I was soon able to read; and with these, two or three books of arithmetic, which my mother procured for me; and it was she that taught me to write, taught me the first five or six rules of arithmetic, with something of music.

My first attempts in poetry were in Welsh, that being the country vernacular, though English was the language of my father's house. In 1770, my best of mother died; I was then, though twenty three years of age, as ignorant of the world almost as a new-born child. This I gradually found by woeful experience; I had worked at my father;' trade since I was nine years of age; but I never, from a child, associated with those of my age, never learned their diversions . I returned every night to my Mother's fire-side, where I talked or read with her; if I ever walked out , it was by myself in unfrequented places, woods, the sea-shore, etc, for I was very pensive, melancholy, and very stupid, as all but my mother thought; when a cheerful fit occurred, it was wild extravagance generally.

After my mother's death, I could no longer be happy at home, where she was never more to be seen. I rambled for some years over a great part of England and Wales; my studies were, during this time, chiefly Architecture, and the other sciences that my trade required. In 1773, I went into Kent, where I stayed for near four years. I had been two or three years in London, Bristol etc. A return to rural objects had a pleasing and powerful effect on my mind; this, and meeting with Dr Aitkin's Essays on Song-writing which gave me much pleasure, revived my poetical taste, and I wrote many of the pieces contained in these volumes in Kent. In 1777, I returned to London, and soon after into Wales; and a restoration of the scenes of youth preserved and heightened my passion for poetry. In 1781, I married., and gradually, as my family increased, was obliged to decline my hitherto pleasing study. In 1790, the general election supplied me with an occasion to scribble some trifles which introduced my verses into some notice, and I was encouraged to print them by subscription. I thus became supplied with every would-be literary fool's apology for exposing myself to public ridicule, the Advice of Friends. This I imagine is more than enough of my history; it is of no importance to anyone to know how many stones I hewed, or on how many grave-stones I have inscribed vile doggrel. Anecdotes of original impressions on the human mind may be of some philosophical use; and I have here honestly given my own. Unavoidable egotisms will be pardoned.

I repeat once more, that there is not in these volumes a single line or epithet that is not my own; whenever a fault has been pointed out , or an improvement suggested, the removal of one, and the accomplishment of the other, was always my own attempt; for, as I before observed, I would not impose of the public on one hand, and I would exercise my own faculties on the other. Corrections and improvements by superior learning and abilities have been said to have taken place in some productions of self-cultivated genius that have appeared; this is very reprehensible; Philosophers read these things, and they should not be deceived , for the sake of investigating the properties and powers of the human mind under all circumstances, advantages and disadvantages, rather than for any intrinsic merit than these, our crude scribblings possess.

Some of my best pieces are still unprinted, as I could not in time recover copies from those to whom I had lent them, not having kept duplicates. I am sorry for this, but I cannot help it; my best pieces were certainly due to my subscribers; but to delay the work longer could not be done with any propriety.

The Etymology of Britain, in one of my notes, is my own; and, I will venture to say, the true one: indeed, this has been very freely acknowledged by the best Welsh critics; yet, very strange, ! it has never before appeared, unless lately from my communications. I have, in several places, aimed at rectifying some mistakes by modern Welsh Historians, gentlemen (if they can be so called) of no conscience, who are partial to everything except Truth. The true history of the Ancient Welsh Bards is willfully suppressed in favour of the wildest preconceptions and absurdist theories that could ever enter the brain of the most barbarous Goth!

I have some general, but no personal, satire; there is too much Priestcraft amongst every sect; too much Kingcraft in all, even republican, governments; yet there are many good priests; and I believe, a brace of good kings may be found; at least I will venture on one.

I have always, with an ancient Briton's warm pride, preserved the freedom of my thoughts, and the independence of my mind: these shall not be subjected to anything save my own conscience. Wherever I meet with scoundralism, though captained by howsoever great a name, my pen shall have all the liberty of my sentiments; I possess a trade, and, in that, independence. I doubt not that numberless errors of judgement may be found in some things that I have written. Other things may be deemed imprudent; but prudence and conscience never walk hand in hand.

The merits that my poems possess is very little indeed, but I hope that they have no taint of that immorality that sweeps, a powerful deluge, over the world; I have declared myself the friend of Peace, Benevolence, Liberty, and the transcendentally lovely Christian religion. Why is it presumptuous in me to hope that my sentiments may diffuse for a little while a feeble glimmer of glow-worm light over a very small part of the world? Who knows that in the bright constellation of stars of the first magnitude that now illumine the Horizon of Truth, I may be one of the feeblest; at least I would not for the world be a cloud in it; to these sentiments I have sacrificed more than can yet be made known of that vile infernal stuff called Prudence, that, though misnomered a virtue, is always infallibly characteristic of a knave or a slave.

The account of the Bardic Triads was drawn up in great haste, and under anxieties that admitted of no cool attention; this was, at the desire of some friends, substituted in the room of the poems that were intended originally; I too late observe it full of inaccuracies and blockheadisms. The originals of these Triads are in the Silurians (which is the most ancient) dialect and orthography. I mention this to obviate the carpings of those who, properly speaking, know no dialect. The Silurian differs in many particulars from the Biblical dialect of modern writers. To attempt an investigation of the true sense of the very obscure term 'Abred' would have required a longer dissertation than I had room for; and, probably. My abilities would have failed me.

I have in one passage mentioned a qualified sense in which Christian Bards and Druids believed in Metempsychosis; this was, that the depraved soul of man passes in a state beyond the grave into progressive modes of existence corresponding with the natures of Earthly worms and brutes, into whom, in a literal sense, the Aboriginal or Patriarchal Druids believed it passed. Taliesin places this probationary, divestigating, or purifying, Metempyschosis, in the Hell Of Christianity, whence the soul gradually rises again to Felicity, the way for it having been opened by Jesus Christ; for, this is his obvious meaning, (from the Welsh): 'Multitudes were ignorant of their state, in Hell, in the miserable progression of deliverance, during the world's five ages; until released by Christ from the captivities of the immense deep, of the abyss of 'Abred'; all those God has taken into his protection.'

I have some thoughts of translating all the bardic Triads; should such an intention be encouraged by the public opinion of the short extracts here given, I will in the course of the ensuing summer, with Permission of Providence, give my translation with the originals to the Press.

I wish that it had been in my power to discharge more fully my very great obligations to a generous public to my subscribers in particular, my real patrons; perhaps, but I care not. I may be a little tautological in attempting to express my gratitude; I have nothing to render but there feeble attempts.

External appearances are such that many are supposed to be my friends who have been in reality very much my foes; but the world must remain undeceived; I am not inclined to publish truths that will involve me in a torrent of misrepresentation, obloquy, and abuse; there are many that 'will never pardon me for the injuries they have done me' . Such is my case; and where is that man who, being a little advanced in life has not experienced much of what is very similar; more than will be prudent for him, if he loves peace, ever to publish? Could I with propriety, boast of any part of my conduct in life, it should be that in particular which has excited the envy, and, of course, the Enmity of some who will better than the public at large understand what I here allude to. If any sentiment or trait in my very humble productions should procure me some friendship, or some favourable opinion of me from the Public, I freely confess that my happiness will very much be increased. If anything of this nature comes from the Good, I shall care nothing for what of a different kind I may experience from what in the vulgar acceptation we call 'Great.''

London, Jan 1ˢᵗ, 1794

'The Mythology of the Ancient Bards' (composed in the Manner of Taliesin) 'recited on Primrose Hill at a Meeting of British Bards, on the summer Solstice of 1792 and ratified at the subsequent Autumn Equinox and Winter Solstice':

The Patriarchical religion of Ancient Britain, called Druidism, but by the Welsh commonly Barddas, (Bardism) though they also term it Derwyddoniaeth, (Druidism) is no more inimical to Christianity than the religion of Noah, Job, or Abraham: - it has never, as some imagine, been quite extinct in Britain; the Welsh Bards have through all ages, down to the present, kept it alive: there is in my possession a manuscript synopsis of it by Llewelyn Sion, a Bard, written about the year 1560; its truth and accuracy are corroborated by innumerable notices, and allusions-in our Bardic manuscripts of every age up to Taliesin in the sixth century, whose poems exhibit a complete system of Druidism by these (undoubtedly authentic) writings it will appear that the ancient British Christianity was strongly tinctured with Druidism. The old Welsh bards kept up a perpetual war with the Church of Rome, and from it experienced much persecution. Narrow understandings may conceive that they were the less Christians for having been Druids. The doctrine of metempsychosis is that which of all others most clearly " ... vindicates the ways of God to Man."'

It is sufficiently countenanced by many passages in the New Testament, and was believed by many of the Primitive Christians, and by the Essenes amongst the Jews.

How truly ridiculous to an Ancient British Mythologist, appears the Bard of Gray with its savage Scandinavian Mythology; the same may be said of other English poems, that, except in this particular, possess the highest poetical excellence.

I cannot help thinking that the British Bardic Mythology would supply poetry with many new ideas, and much of very pleasing imagery; it seems to me far more rational, sublime and congenial to Human Nature, than the superlatively barbarous and bloody Theology of the Edda, which so m e depraved imaginations are to be charmed with.

There are in the world writers of matchless impudence - these will, without knowing a word of the Welsh language, without having seen one of its many thousands of manuscripts, arrogantly tell the public that what is here said of Bardism is all a fiction, just as if a man, without knowing anything of of the Greek language, should peremptorily tell us that such persons as Homer, Pindar, or Aristotle, never existed, or that the writings attributed to these great men are gross impositions on the credulity of mankind.

The following preliminary aphorisms are thought necessary:

1. All animated beings originate in the lowest point of existence (Annwn), whence, by a regular gradation, they rise higher and higher in the scale of excellence till they arrive at the highest state of happiness and perfection that is possible for finite beings.

2. All the states of animation below that of humanity are necessarily evil;; and where Evil unavoidably preponderates, no being can, consistent with Justice, be deemed culpable, nor are they objects of punishment, - here Fate reigns.

3. Beings, as their souls, by passing from ferocious to more gentle and harmless animals, approach the state of Humanity, become ameliorated in their dispositions, less influenced by Evil, and attain to some degree of negative goodness.

4. Every being is destined to fill an allotted place in the creation, and endues with those sensibilities, benign propensities, and mental capacities, that are requisite to render him happy in that station, which he never can be in any other lastingly, and to this the Creator will finally bring him.

5. Beings, having been led up through such a succession of animal existences are as necessary to unfolding their defined character, and preparing them for their ultimate office in the Creation, arrive at the state of Humanity, where Good and Evil are so frequently balanced, that Liberty takes place, the Will becomes Free; whence Man becomes accountable for his actions, having 0 power of attaching himself either to the Good or the Evil as he may, or may not, subject his propensities to the control of Reason and unsophisticated Nature, these being the fixed laws of the Creator.

6. Man being possessed of Liberty has the power of co-acting with the Deity, and of attaching himself to Good, and by persevering in this course till death arises to such a state above Humanity as corresponds with his accessions of Goodness, and with that degree in which they preponderate against Evil.

7. In all the states of existence above Humanity Good preponderates, and therein all Beings are necessarily good; hence they can never fall, but are still advancing higher and higher in the scale of happiness and perfection, till they arrive at their final destination, where every being, in his allotted place, will be completely happy to all Eternity, without the possibility of ever falling into Evil; and, being convinced that he could not possibly be equally happy in any other station, will never have any desire to quit that wherein he is.

8. Man, attaching himself to Evil, falls in Death into such an animal state of existence as corresponds with the turpitude of his soul, which may be to great as to call him down into the lowest point of existence, whence he shall again return through such a succession of animal existences as are more proper to divest him of his evil propensities; After traversing such a course (ireiglo'r Abred), he will again rise to the state of Humanity, whence, according to contingencies, he may rise or fall, yet should he fall he shall again rise; and, should this happen for millions of ages, the path of happiness is still open to him, and will so remain to all eternity; for, sooner or later, whence he he will infallibly arrive at his destined station of happiness, whence he never falls. Eternal Misery is a thing impossible; it cannot possibly consist with the attributes of God, who is never actuated by malevolent resentment that proceeds from a display of superior power, which originates in Pride. God is Love in the most positive and unlimited degree; he resist Evil for the sake of annihilating it,

and not for the
more malevolent purpose of punishing.

9. Finite beings can never comprehend Infinity; they cannot conceive anything of God, but as something external to themselves individually different, and, consequently, finite. The Deity for this reason, though in himself infinite, manifests himself to finite comprehensions as a finite being, as in the Person of Jesus Christ, etc.

10. The ultimates states of Happiness are eternally undergoing the most delightful renovations in endless succession, without which no Finite Being could ever, consistent with happiness, endure the tedium of Eternity. These renovations will not, like the deaths of the lower states of existence, occasion a suspension of memory and consciousness of self-identity.

11. Memory, and the consciousness of having transgressed the Laws of God, are suffered to remain sometimes in the lower states of existences after death, as a temporary punishment, and for implanting in them an aversion to Evil.

12. Man, on arriving at a state above Humanity, recovers the perfect recollection of all his former modes of existence, and to eternity retains it. It is this, and this only, that constitutes a Being's consciousness of having been, and of still being, ever since its first creation, through all states of animated existences; identically one and the same: he could not otherwise say to himself, I was the Animal, I was the Man, or any other being, that at such a period, passed, lived, acted, felt and experienced in such a manner: without this perpetuation of conscious memory, death would be absolute annihilation, and not a change in the mode of existence: without this, a being in any superior state would be a new Creature, and not a continuance of a former.

13. No knowledge can but be acquired but by experience - to obtain all possible knowledge, it is necessary to pass through all possible modes of existence, and to experience all that is peculiarly known to everyone of these, each of them affording such a supply of knowledge that no other possibly can. Man in the states of happiness recovers the memory of all that he observed and experienced in every mode of existence through which he has passed.

14. All the knowledge that in the state of Humanity we have of supernal existence has been communicated by Celestial Beings, who, of their own Benevolence, subjected to that of the Deity, return for a while to this world to inform man of what is necessary for him to know of his duty, and of what constitutes happiness in this and in future states, and what, by perseverance in Virtue, he may hope for, and be assured of. Knowledge of this kind has thus been communicated to man in all parts of the world, though more eminently so, by the Jewish Prophets and Jesus Christ, in whom all that can be comprehended of the Deity by Finite Beings was, and in him will eternally be, manifested. Bardism always refers to its origin to Divine communications, and never talked of, I know not what, Religion of Nature.

15. The propensities of animals to prey upon, and destroy, each other is a regulation of Divine Benevolence for expediting the progress of beings through their several destined modes of existence to the states of happiness.

16. Man subjecting himself to death in the cause of Truth, Justice and Virtue, and for these, foregoing all the enjoyments of this world, and life itself, does the most meritorious act of goodness that he possibly can; and thus, attaching himself to the highest degree of virtue and holiness, passes by death to the highest and ultimate state of Celestial Felicity.

17. Man, having been guilty of crimes that are punishable by Death, must be so punished; and by giving himself up a voluntary victim to Death, being conscious of deserving it, does all that lies in his power to compensate for his crimes; attaches himself to the greatest degree of good that he possibly can, by giving up all of life and its enjoyments, by suffering, voluntarily, all that ought to be inflicted on him, for his transgression; he by such a Death passes to the highest state of happiness.

18. The sacrifice of animals, which were always those of the least ferocity of disposition, was a religious co-operation with Divine Benevolence, by raising such an animal up to the state of Humanity, and consequently expediting his progress towards felicity, it was not to appease, we know not what, Divine wrath, a thing that cannot possibly exist; the idea of which is, of all others, the most blasphemously disgraceful to the Deity.

19. Man must not, but from an absolute necessity to save his own life, commit depredations on any animated beings, or kill then to gratify wanton propensities, he must never inflict death or torture but in cases of self-preservation, not of sensual Indulgence, or of malevolent animosity. No inferior being destroys another, but to save his own life, which he cannot otherwise possibly do. Man must govern himself by the same Law of Nature, which is that of God.

20. Man cannot possibly commit any act that is not more or less conducive to the general and ultimate good; he, though it is forbidden to him, by wantonly killing an innocent creature, removes it to a higher state of existence, and consequently benefits it; on a similar plan has God infallibly secured much more than an ample recompense for all the wrongs that any being may suffer from another.

21. Fortitude is the greatest and first of all virtues; without it, no other virtue can be practised; what we do from the excitements of pleasure and self-gratification is not, or but a very inferior kind of, Virtue. We can never unequivocally evince our love of Virtue, Justice, Benevolence, or any thing else, but by suffering willingly for its sake. Without fortitude we shrink from all that is good and laudable, if with it any, even the least, degree of suffering is connected. The commission of all Vice proceeds from the fear of practising its opposite, Virtue.

22. Pride is the utmost degree of human depravity; it supplies the motive for perpetrating every kind of wickedness, it aims at Superiority and Power, which none but God is, of right, entitled to. Man may confer conditionally, and for the general good, a well restrained and limited power on superior merit; but none are entitled to usurp it. Self-created superiority, and power over others is a dethroning of the Almighty, as far as man can do it. Pride is the destroyer (cythraul) of the works of the Creator, the subverter of all order, forces itself obtrusively into a station that was never allotted to it. All men are equal in the Creator's paternality, as his children: and to superior worth and virtue he has secured infallibly the approbation of the truly Good and Wise, who will ever voluntarily exalt it to its merited height if not frustrated by the Proud, who always, and often with temporary success, aim at usurping what is only due to transcendent Virtues and Beneficent Abilities: Pride casts down into the lowest point of existence.

23. The fouls is an inconceivable minute particle of the most refined matter, is necessarily endued with life, and never dies; but at the dissolution of one body, it passes into another higher or lower in the scale of existence, where it expands itself into that form and corporiety which its acquired propensities necessarily give it, or of that animal (with whose body it becomes clothed) wherein only such propensities can possibly reside naturally. - By the way, let us ask what modern philosophers, or rather anti-philosophers, mean by unembodied and immaterial beings or spirits, existing either in happiness or misery? if any thing can be understood of Immateriality it must be Nonentity; mere Nothing; unless we conceive it to be the Deity, who is infinite, which immateriality also is, and cannot be divided or limited. We cannot possibly conceive any idea of a Finite Intelligent Being, without annexing to it something (however subtile and refined) like materiality.

24. Liberty once obtained will never be lost; it consists in a perfect knowledge of the causes of Evil in every mode of existence, and of all the operative principles of Nature. Permanently perfect Liberty can never universally take place till all Beings and Modes of existence are entirely divested of their Evils.

25. The state of Humanity being that of Liberty is the only State of Probation; it is, for that reason, on the actions of this state only that Divine Judgment will be passed.

26. The Creation is still in its Infancy; God will, by the progressive operations of his Providence, bring all Beings to the point of Liberty (which is the Human State) wherein only, even by God himself, Evil can be combated and subdues; wherein all power begins, exists, and subsists.

27. Evil, and all its causes, once perfectly known, which it cannot be till all beings have passed through all possible Modes of finite existence, will be for ever hated and avoided; but, being in itself possible, it will, with all other possibilities, eternally exist in its abstract principles, all possibilities are things of eternity.

28. All Modes of existence which are necessarily as numerous as Divine Conception can make them, will for ever remain in existence with no other change than that of being thoroughly divested of all their Evils, and continue eternally as beautiful varieties in the Creation, which without this numerosity of externalities would not possess perfect beauty.

29. All the various Modes of existence, for ever externally the same, will, when internally divested of all Evils, be occupied successively by Celestials, or those that inhabit the Circle of Felicity, these, amongst other changes, will vary and delightfully relieve what would otherwise be insupportable in Eternity to finite Beings. All these Modes of Existence will, when purged of their Evils, be equally perfect, equally happy, equal in the general estimation, and equally fathered by the Creator. Peace, Love and ineffable benignity filling the whole creation. All mental and corporeal affections and propensities of benign tendency will remain for ever, and constitute the joys of the Celestial existencies.

30. Our infallible rule of Duty is, not to do or desire any thing but what can eternally be done and obtained in the Celestial states, wherein no Evil can exist. The Good and Happiness of one Being, must not arise from the Evil, or misery, of another.

Such are the outlines of Bardism, Druidism, or the ancient British Philosophy, at least of what it is, as refined 'by Christianity, in which the Bards adopted nothing that was averse to their Ancient Theology, but what rather . confirmed the truth of it.

Christianity at its early introduction into Britain about the year 62, found nothing' in Druidism inconsistent with its own doctrines, if we admit (which, perhaps, in a qualified sense, with the Christian Bards, we may) the doctrine of the Metempsychosis.

The Bards or Druids continued for many centuries after they became Christians, the Minister of Religion, even till, and probably in some places long after, the time of the two Athanasian and incipiently Popish Bishops, Germanus and Lupus; this is pretty evident from our oldest and most authentic manuscripts. The Bards have through all ages considered themselves as a properly qualified Priesthood or Ministrators of Religion. Much more might be said on this subject, which~either room nor propriety admit of in this place.

IOLO'S notes on 'POEMS LYRICAL and PASTORAL,' IN ENGLISH

Wales equals 'Cymru':
The Welsh have always called themselves 'Cymru': the strictly literal meaning of the word is 'Aborigine'; they are the 'Cimbri,' or 'Cimmeri', of the ancients, and have been distinguished by this appellation in all ages, and in all countries, wherever they have appeared, from Asia Minor to Great Britain, as if they considered themselves the Aborigines of the world ; their language they call Cymraeg, that is, aboriginal, or primitive language; for the word cannot possibly admit of any other meaning; there is something very remarkable in this; but on it we cannot venture to found any conjecture; in this age of the world it is too lat; for time has long thrown into deep oblivion the origin of every nation and language. The Welsh, however, in this, their national appellation, derived from the remotest antiquity, may find pretentions of some plausibility, to a far nobler origin, than that of being descendants of a gang of scoundrels who came from Troy to Britain, through many countries, on a plundering expedition. Some derive 'Cymry' or Cimbri, from the Patriarch Gomer, a wild conjecture, a groundless etymology – let them study the Cimbric language!

A further Note on 'Cimbric':
'Cimbric' is the primeval and general name of all the Celtic nations, by which in all ages, from earliest antiquity, they were known; and by which the Welsh, to this day, call themselves, and have done so uninterruptedly from the remotest times. The term 'Cambrian' is derived from Geoffrey of Monmouth's fable of 'Camber,' who, if we believe him, was the third son of Brutus.

The Temper of the Welsh:
The Ancient Britons were noted for their warmth of temper; hence the proverbial phrase, 'of Welsh blood!'

The White-washed Houses of Glamorgan:

'It has, from very remote antiquity, been the custom in Glamorgan to white-wash the houses, not only the insides, but the outsides also; and even the barns, stables, walls of yards and gardens. In a very ancient poem attributed to Aneurin, it says,' In Glamorgan people are courteous and gentle, Married women are honoured and the walls are white.'

Dafydd ap Gwilym, a bard that flourished about 1350, says, 'This Bard loves this beautiful country, its wines and its white homes.'

Mr Strutt, from Diodorus Siculus, says that the Britons white-washed their houses with chalk.' (Chronicle of England) From hence it appears that the Welsh of Glamorgan retain a very ancient British custom.

The Depravity of City Dwellers:

The moral principles of the inhabitants of overgrown towns are, almost necessarily, highly depraved; at least this is the case of a great majority of them; the present enormous magnitude of London, besides being the premature grave of our drained dominions, harbours such a vast number of villains that, ranked at the heels of one possessed of all the fanaticism of Lord George Gordon, with the good sense and cool deliberation of Oliver Cromwell, would soon spread desolation over the whole island. The legislature will, when, probably too late, find this to be true.

The Drowned Canton:

A very large tract of fenny country on this coast (Cardiganshire) was, about the year 500AD, overflown by the sea, occasioned by the carelessness of those who kept the flood-gates; as we are informed by Taliesin, the famous bard, in a poem of his still extant. There were, it is said , many large towns, a great number of villages and places of noblemen, in this canton; and amongst them the Palace of Gwyddno Garanhir, a petty Prince of the country. There were lately (and I believe are still) to be seen in the sands of this Bay, large stones with inscriptions on them, the characters Roman, but the language unknown. This disastrous circumstance is recorded by many other ancient Welsh writers.

Welsh Mariners:
St Cyric is the patron Saint of Welsh mariners.

Pilgrimages:
It was usual for those (even females), who went from North Wales on pilgrimages to St David's,
to pass the dangerous strands, and sail over the rough bays in slight coracles, without any one to assist them; so firmly were they persuaded that their adored sant, as well as St Cyric, the ruler of the waves, would protect them in all dangers.

The Popes:
Words of the Old Monk:
'Would haughty Popes your senses bubble,
And once to Rome your steps entice;
'Tis quite as well, and saves some trouble,
Go visit old saint Taffy twice!
The Welsh Bards most respectful compliments to their infallible Holiness the Popes of all sects and denominations (for such there certainly are), and hopes they will pardon him for not giving a closer version of the good old monk's jingling line (above) assures them that he has not taken greater liberties with it than what they take daily with the Bible (and indeed with all Truth in general) well-knowing that it will not fully answer their laudable purposes without a little *decent* perversion.

Penlline Castle:
Penlline Castle is the property of Miss Gwinette, who has lately built an elegant new house, in the castle stile, close to the ruin. She has shown her good taste in not demolishing the old castle, some of the walls of which are constructed in the manner of the old Roman walls of Segontium, by the town of Caernarvon.

The Line of Beauty:
The author was, one evening, invited to be of a party to see the new-laid-out pleasure grounds of a Gentleman. The walks waved regularly along the rectilinear fences with very minute spirality, and crossed

the ground at right angles, dividing the laboriously–levelled lawn into parts exactly square and equal. Clumps of pine and flowering shrubs, of studied rotundity, bestudded the smooth-shaven green at regular distances; and the stiffest formalities prevailed everywhere. The Gardener, who attended, talked much of 'the Line of Beauty.'

'Curse this Line of Beauty,' I exclaimed.

'You must write a song on the subject,' said one of the Ladies.

'By God, you must!' cried a young Clergyman, 'and the words 'the Line of Beauty' must   conclude every stanza. Find rhymes if you can!'

"I insist on it!'said another Lady,' and I think your Reverend swearer should have a conspicuous place in the song.'

After an hour's retirement, I rejoined the good-humoured company with all my verses at the ready!

The Nightingale:
The Nightingale sings by day as well as by night. It is rather strange that this fact has not been observed by any of our English poets.

On Pastoral Poetry:
The author thinks Pastoral a species of Poetry that admits of as great a variety of subjects as any other whatsoever; and that it is not necessary, in the manner of modern Poets, to confine it solely to Love, and make his 'whining swains' ring perpetual changes on the names of, 'hard-hearted Phillis,' or 'cold Amarillis,' etc.' A poet in the character of a Shepherd, an occupation most proper of all others to represent primeval simplicity and virtue, describes objects a as they naturally present themselves to the senses, and affect the mind; or utter sentiments that spring from the simple notions and inborn feelings of those that are unacquainted with the abstractions of philosophy, and the complex ideas derived from art. The Shepherd, who is the representative and pupil of Nature, has, for his rural song, at least as great a diversity as the more philosophic rhimer can boast of; who if he pleases, may take to himself all the fine things of art, provided he leave the sylvan Bard in full possession of Nature.

There are some Critics, as Dr Johnson observed, (and the cap often fits his own head), 'who love to talk of what they do not know,' that affect to ridicule Pastoral Poetry; their misconceptions of its nature are, most probably, occasioned by the absurd and unnatural rhapsodies that many have given us under the name of 'Pastoral'; the sentiments highly fantastical, with descriptions of what no climate of this globe affords but that of Grub Street; where, among many rare things, are to be seen, the violet of March and the rose of June blowing at the same time, as we are told by Mr Pope, in his First Pastoral.

It would, perhaps, be not amiss if our modern Critics and Poets would take into consideration the maxims of the Welsh Bards from their Poetic Triads, given below.

Have any of the Poets, from the days of Aristotle to the present time, ever said anything more to the purpose in these Triads? But these Triads, which contain some of the most just, because the most natural, rules of criticism that are to be met with in any language, will never emerge from their deep obscurity in the Welsh language, until they are translated. Find them below in this volume for the very first time.

Further Observations on the Pastoral:

The Reader will observe, that the term 'Lyric Pastoral,' has often been used, and will perhaps ask for what reason? It is this – we often observe shepherds, and other rural characters, diverting themsleves with songs which are always in the proper sense of the word, sung to a tune; the verse of course must be 'Lyric'; Shenstone's Pastoral Ballads are, for this reason, amongst others, far more natural than the Bucolics of Virgil. Many more of our poets could be named – this, at least, is a Welsh Bard's opinion, who admits of no other authority but that of Nature. We often hear the fields rebound with 'Chevy Chase,' 'Tweed Side' songs, and the like. But we never hear them spouting 'Heroics'; and it is thus in every part of Britain. But some, it seems, are of opinion that we should write for other countries, climates, and times, rather than solely our own. Bravo, to my good Critics!

On Wheat and the Modern Poets:
The wheat's bloom is a beautiful, and very interesting, rural object; though but little noticed by modern Poets.

Ivor the Generous:
Ivor the Generous was Lord of Baseleg, in the County of Monmouth. Ivor lived about the middle of the fourteenth century, and was celebrated by the Bards of his Age, and of all succeeding ages, for his unexampled liberality. He was the warm Patron of Dafydd ap Gwilym, whose poetry today is still held in the highest estimation.

The Bard as Peacemaker:
It was not lawful for the Bards to bear arms; or for anyone to beat a naked weapon in their presence.

The Most Famous Welshman:
Arthur, after all the fables that have been told by Geoffrey of Monmouth, and a thousand more, was no more than the son of Meirig, the King of Glamorgan, elected to the chief Command of the British armies against the Saxons, as appears from the ancient register of the Cathedral Church of Llandaff, and many old books of pedigrees in the Welsh language still extant; which are to the unprejudiced of much better authority than the Romance of Geoffrey. One that Impartiality consults some genuine fragments of history, that are to be met with in Wales, will be much inclined to think that the ancient Britons were never united under one hereditary Sovereign Monarch of their own nation; the island of Britain was always divided into a great many petty principalities, that, when occasion required, elected temporary commanders-in-chief to lead their armies in cases of invasion. Such was Arthur, and others. This opinion will however have no great weight with some Welshmen, who love their own country better than the Truth.

The Bard and the Birds:
About the year 1768, the Author, with two or three more, found a great number of swallows, in a torpid state, clinging in clusters to each other, by their bills, in a cave of the sea cliffs, near Dunraven

Castle, in the County of Glamorgan. They revived after they had been some hours in a warm room but died in a day or two after, though all possible care had been taken of them.

The Bard's Home River:
The Dawon, a river of Glamorgan, that, running through the town of Cowbridge, and by the village of Plimpton, the Author's place of abode, falls into the Severn Sea at, and forms the harbour of, Abertawe.

Other Famous Bards, 1, Aneirin:
Aneurin was a celebrated Bard of the sixth century. He was called Myderin Beirdd, king of the Bards. He was brother of the celebrated scholar monk Gildas. Aneirin's poem 'Gododdin,' a noble heroic Poem, the first for poetical sublimity in the Welsh language, is still extant; it is equally distinguished for the fine pathos of numberless passages, and is of considerable length; the subject of the poem is the battle of Catraeth, fought by the Britons against the Saxons; Gildas was, like his brother Aneirin, a Bard; and fragments of his work are still with us; there were two more of the bothers who were Bards, Ceian and Avan; and, in a manuscript in my possession, their brothers and sisters, to the number of twenty-four in the whole, sons and daughters of Caw o Brydyn, are said to have been Bards; and what is more wonderful, they were also saints! – as monks were so called in those times in Wales. This Caw o Brydyn was a petty Prince of the Ortadini, in North Britain; and having been driven out of his territories by the Saxons, he retreated into Wales with his sons and daughters, who thereupon entered upon a monastic life; the ese 'saints' were of the Monastery of St Illtus; it would have been natural for them to remain together as much as possible.

Other Famous Bards, 2, Taliesin:
Taliesin lived in the 5th century. He professed himself a Druid; and, in many of his poems, gives an ample display of the doctrines of metempsychosis (transmigration of souls) and other druidical opinions. He very much enriched Welsh poetry by introducing into it the Roman versification, the hexameter, pentameter, the saphic,

and other metres, till then strangers to the Welsh language. These have ever since been retained by the Cambrian Bards; and are, I believe, unknown to every other modern tongue. O! for another Taliesin to teach us the sublime Muse, those truly musical and majestic numbers. Surely this may be done!

A Famous British Warrior:

Caractacus was the famous ancient British Prince of the Silures of South Wales; who, after nobly withstanding all the Roman force in Britain for nine years, was, at last, by treachery only, subdued and carried a prisoner of war to Rome, where his magnanimous speech before the Emperor Claudius, procured him his liberty. Some families in South Wales claim a lineal descent from him.

Meugant and Merlin:

Meugant lived in the fourth century and was preceptor to the celebrated Merlin, according to one of our ablest Welsh antiquaries, who, in the time of Queen Elizabeth, was Archdeacon of Merioneth. There are still extant some poems of Meugant as well as his disciple Merlin; and from those pieces we clearly perceive, that they were neither prophets nor conjurors themselves: they were honest Welsh Bards, who recorded in verse the occurrences of their own times, never troubling themselves with futurity; but they suffer a little from counterfeiting, interpolating, and other vile scribblers. Dear P.....n, thou Jack Ketch of the literary community, pray tuck up these idle rascals, or flog them with severest lash at the cart's tail; attempt not, however, like thy namesake at Tyburn, for the sordid sake of gain to catch all indiscriminately in thy noose; do not approach our venerable bards till thou art able to converse in their own language.

'The Guardians of Celestial Truth' – the Bards and Druids

The Truth was held so sacred by the ancient British bards and Druids that they would never admit into their poetical compositions anything whatever of a fictious nature;; their fundamental maxim was to search for Truth, with the most rigid severity; hence in all the genuine works still extant of our ancient Welsh bards, from

Meugant, about the close of the fourth century, to the present time, we meet not with a single poem founded on fiction; and, singular as it might appear, contrary to the practice of all other nations,, the most authentic histories of the Welsh are in verse, and all their fabulous writings in prose. Some have asserted, in their vindication of that grand Romancer Geoffrey of Monmouth, that the Trojan origin of the Welsh is mentioned by Taliesin; but this is one of the most glaring falsehoods that was ever uttered; for I defy all the world to produce from the poems of that noble bard, or of any other whatever, of acknowledged authenticity , one single word alluding in the least to any such event; none of the Bards contemporary with Geoffrey , or of any age prior to him, make the least mention of any such thing; but Truth, in general, is made to give way to blind national vanity by most of our Welsh historians, who have by these unwarrantable assertions, brought the authenticity of our old poetical manuscripts under some suspicion, by charging Taliesin and others, with Geoffrey's glaring lies.

Bards of Peace:

The bard was peculiarly the Herald of peace; he, clad in his uni-coloured robe, emblematic of Truth and peace, presented himself between the two armies just on the point of engaging, and all instantly laid down their arms, giving thus the Peace-Maker an opportunity, which was often successful, of reconciling the contending parties, and removing all their anomalies; the Bards; appearance, in this official robe and character, operated in the same manner, as the modern flag of truce; we are told by Diodorus that this was effected by, I know not what, wonderful powers of enchanting song; and this romantic fable has been pretty well hackneyed by many modern writers who have favoured, or, rather, preferred, the world with their very curious histories of the old Welsh Bards.

The Bards of Britain were the first who avowed themselves as the Heralds of Peace; in the Christian world, the first that literally converted their spears into ploughshares, and their swords to pruning hooks, learning war no more, that appeared in Britain.

The Authenticity of the Works of the Ancient Bards of Britain:

There is nothing in the Welsh poetic taste, however defective in other respects it may appear, which absurdly derives from the mythology, sentiments, and scenery, of the Greek and Roman Poets, but all is the natural growth of Britain!

Songs of War:

The ancient Britons had their war-songs, and a variety of them adapted to various occasions; of these we have many still extant in manuscripts; they are for the most part in triplets, which kind of verse is called 'the warrior's triplet.'

Bards of civilization:

The original intention of the Bardic Institution was to promote civilization. The primitive meaning of the word 'Bard' is 'Priest'; 'Prydydd' is the most common Welsh word for 'Poet'; the literal sense of which, as near as it can be rendered, is, 'Embellisher,' 'Regulator,' 'Reformer' or 'Polisher.'

The Living Bards:

According to Julius Caesar, the ancient Welsh writers, and the traditions retained by the bards, the Druidic Institutions originated in Britain; it is not yet extinct, for we have in Wales, a small number still remaining in an uninterrupted succession from the ancient British Bards and Druids. A Welsh Bard of the present age retains the ancient title of Bardd wrth Fraint a Dafod Beirdd Ynys Prydain; in English, 'Bard according to the Rights and Institutes of the Bards of the Island of Britain,'; The Druidic Theology also remains in Wales, where it was never entirely abolished; yet Druidism has been fought for everywhere but in Wales and the Welsh langauuge, where it is only to be found.

Ceremonies of the Bards

The Welsh Bards always meet in the open air whilst the sun is above the horizon, where they form a circle of stones, according to ancient custom; this Circle they call the Circle of Concord, or of Confederation. In these days however, it is formed only of a few very small stones, or pebbles, such as may be carried to the spot in one's pocket; but this would not have been deemed sufficient by those who formed the stupendous Bardic Circle of Stonehenge.

The Bardic Circle:

The Bardic Circle, or Druidic Temple, as some call it, wherein the bards meet, is formed of stones called 'white stones', or 'stones of testimony' and in the middle there is the 'presidial stone', by all but the Bards called an 'altar.'

The Solemn Days of Bardism:

The four grand and solemn days are, of ancient usage, the two equinoxes, and the two solstices; the new and full moons are also, subordinately, solemn bardic days. These are the conspicuous days, we may say 'holidays,' of Nature, and were, doubtless, observed long before the institution of any other solemn, sabbatical, or festival days. This, and many other usages of the Ancient British Bards, bear the stamp of, and are, obviously retained from, remotest antiquity. These customs are not known to have been discontinued or suspended in any age whatever, but have always, to the present day, been observed. This is a matter of no less curiosity than of wonder, that it should not have long ago been noticed; but Ancient British Bardism has for ages been in the hands of those who ranked not in the higher classes, and is retained only in those very sequestered and mountainous places that are seldom, if ever, visited by literary men. Bardism has also been for time immemorial under some degree of persecution; its regular proffessors are known in Glamorgan by the nick-name 'Gwyr Cwm y felin,' and generally supposed to be infidels, conjurors, and we know not what. The North Walian Bards, as they call themselves, but improperly, of whose meetings we sometimes of late meet with accounts, know nothing at all of the ancient and genuine Bardism. The Bards of the Druidic order wore uni-coloured robes of white, emblematic of Truth, which was, figuratively, said to be of the colour of light, or the Sun; and uni-coloured, or in every thing, time and place, one and the same thing.

The Beliefs of the Bards:
The Bards and Druids believed in metempsychosis; in which the depraved soul of man passes in a state beyond the grave into progressive modes of existence, corresponding with the natures of the earthly worms and brutes, into whom, in the literal sense, the Aboriginal or Patriarchical Druids, believed it passed. Taliesin places this probationary, divestigating., or purifying, metempsychosis, in the Hell of Christianity, whence the soul gradually rises again to felicity. As
Taliesin has it, 'the multitudes were ignorant of their state in Hell, in the miserable progression of deliverance, during the world's five ages; until released from the captivities of the immense Deep, of the abyss of Abred. All those had God taken into his protection."

The Welsh Epigram:
The chief excellence of the Welsh epigram, in general, like that of the ancient Greeks, does not consist in that silly thing, and 'false pretence to wit', called 'point,' but in a striking idea or sentiment, diffused through the whole.

Welsh Versification:
This little poem, written about the year 1770, is one of the author's first attempts in English poetry, attempting also to try what effect Greek and Roman modes of versification when attempted in the English language; and may not very similar observations be made on national music? a mode of verification much used by the Welsh Poets would have in the English language. This peculiarity consists in making the fourth syllable, whereon the pause lies, of the second, fourth, sixth and eighth, lines of the stanza rhyme to the last syllable of the first, third, fifth, and seventh, lines, instead of making the last syllable of the first and third lines,, etc, rhyme together. This perhaps may not please; it may possibly displease, an English ear; but the reader of Welsh Poetry very much admires it in hi sown , and I believe, no less than in the English, language. The fundamental charm, perhaps, in the poetry of all languages, is no more than a certain something, which, by general custom and frequent usage, has

been familiarized to , and is, consequently, expected or fought after by, the ear. Many of the most approved and harmonious kinds of Welsh verse would found them very strange, and far from agreeable to an Englishman; the same thing, I believe, may be said of the Grammar.

Such are the peculiar idioms of the Welsh language, that, in many passages, a translation, or rendering, of the sentiment, regardless of the verbality, was the most proper attempt.

The Cimbri:

The Cimbri is the primeval and general name of the Celtic nations, by which in all ages, they were known; and by the Welsh, to this day. The term 'Cambrian' is derived from Geoffrey of Monmouth's fable of Camber, who, if we believe him, is the third son of Brutus.

Injuries to the Welsh:

The Welsh still retain a lively sensibility of the numerous injuries that they have, through a long succession of ages, experienced from the Coritani, Belgians, Scots, Picts, Romans, Danes, Saxons and Normans, and complaints of this nature are, to this day, the frequent themes of the ancient British muse.

A 16th century reminder:

'The office or function of the British or Cambrian Bards, is to keep and preserve the Tri Cov Ynys Prydain, the Three Records, or Memorials of Britain (otherwise called the British Antiquities) for the preservation whereof, when the Bards are graduated at their Commencements, they are trebly rewarded.

The first of the three Cov, or Memorials, is:
The history of notable acts of the Princes of Britain,
The language of the Britons (of which the Bards are to give an account of every syllable therein, in order to preserve the ancient language,)
To record the pedigrees, or descents, of the princes, their division of lands, and blazoning of arms.

The Isle of Honey:

Y Fel Ynys, the Isle of Honey was one of the ancient names of Britain, according to the British Triads, one of our oldest, and most authentic, Welsh manuscripts; the other two names are Clas Merddin, which signifies The Highlands in the Sea, or, as some copies have it, Clas Meidden, Hilly Lands or Fields, and, Prydain, the name by which it is at present, and has been for at least 2,000 years, known to the old Britons; though Mr MacPherson says, at random I suppose, that this name was never known to the Welsh; this is one of his very numerous assertions that may be pronounced truly *curious*.

The True Meaning of 'Prydain':

The strict literal meaning of 'Prydain' is 'Beautiful'; nothing can be more obvious than this etymology; it is so demonstrably just that it cannot possibly admit of the lest doubt; and yet, strange as it may appear, it has never hitherto been given by any Welsh Aniquarian or Etymologist whatever; nor has any Welsh Grammarian yet noticed the termination 'ain'; in sense exactly the same as the English 'ful' in 'beautiful, though it ends a great number of words in the language, as, Cyfrain, Dwyrain Owain and many others, some hundreds, perhaps more; with the following names of places: Berain, Cedewain, and many others too; proud of having discovered the true etymology of the name of my highly celebrated native island, that has so long in vain been groped for in the dark, to the astonishment of everyone that has a tolerable knowledge of the Welsh language, I have deviated into what, I fear, will displease some, but others will not disapprove of it. There are but very few countries, perhaps in the world, that, like the word 'Britain,' retain their ancient names in their aboriginal language still living within them, but how little, if any thing, corrupted or altered, antiquaries, whenever they dabble in 'British' or 'Celtic' etymologies, run into the wildest absurdities; but why is it so? There are Welshmen, well skilled in their native language, that would, without any eye to interest, afford those gentlemen any information in their power, and be highly gratified in being called so upon.

Address to the Inhabitants of Wales, exhorting them to Emigrate, with William Penn, to Pennsylvania, to which many Welsh families went.

The rash of intolerant laws that were enacted about this time, and had been, it must be confessed, in some degree, justly provoked, fell, with equal severity on the peaceful and the turbulent, on many of the most loyal as well as seditious; and drove out of the Principality of Wales considerable numbers of people, who, for their loyalty as subjects, and their pacific principles of Christians, were entitled highly to the protection of their country, and even to a degree of indulgence, to which, perhaps, no other party could possibly support any claim.

The Church of England, in those days, under the influence of one of those mistakes that are incidental to everything that originates in human nature, was, it must be confessed, of a persecuting spirit; by this error, it has, long ago, been acknowledged, and reformed; its present moderation is but little short of exemplary; can so much be said of some of its opponent sects?

The Madoucan Tribe of Welsh Native Americans:

Very soon, after the settlement of Virginia and other parts of North America by the English, accounts were received of a tribe of Welsh Indians in interior part of the Continent; and at this time there are, in Wales and America, Welshmen living who have conversed with these people, who are now, as it appears from numerous and well-authenticated accounts, seated on the River Missouri, about five hundred miles above its junction with the Mississippi.

The Origins of the Welsh American Indians:

Many of our Welsh historians assert that America was discovered about the year 1170, by Madoc, son of Owain Gwynedd, Prince of Wales. We have manuscript accounts of this before the birth of Columbus. Dr David Powel, in Queen Elizabeth's time, says, in his History of Wales, that Madoc, in the hopes of discovering the lands that lay beyond the Atlantic, and of finding there a retreat from the horrors of intestine wars which had deluged all Wales with blood, resolved on a voyage of discovery; and, sailing westward, arrived in less than two months, on the coasts of a fine, fertile country, destitute of inhabitants; leaving about one hundred of his men, he returned to Wales, and as soon as possible, set about preparing another fleet for a second expedition; telling his countrymen what a fine country he had discovered, where they might, enjoy liberty, peace and plenty, representing to them, on the other hand, what barren rocks his brethren and nephews were, with hands of murder, contending for; so, having prevailed on many to go with him, he set sail from south Wales with a fleet of ten ships, full of persons of both sexes as preferred peace to discord. This second voyage occurred in the year 1195, according to Sir Thomas Herbert, who, having free access on all occasions to the noble collection of Welsh manuscripts in the library of Ragland Castle, had better opportunities of tracing the history of this remarkable event than any other person living. The total destruction, by fire, of this library has not yet been brought into the list of Oliver Cromwell's glories; it is time, however, that it should. Long! Very long! to Time's remotest period, shall the curse of Welsh Literature attend the detestable name of Oliver Cromwell

The Bible in Welsh and Welsh Conformity:

The Welsh, one would have imagined, had, during the Civil War of Cromwellian sanctity, given the most unequivocal proofs of loyalty, but many of them dissented from the Church of England, which was then inspired by the true spirit of Popery; the Tigers of Religious Persecution were called up from their native hell, their talons fastened indiscriminately on the innocent as well as the guilty, if any guilt could possibly exist in following the dictates of a tender, though, perhaps, mistaken, conscience; dissension was absurdly, or, more probably, maliciously considered, as the grand characteristic of sedition; so, without the least reference to any other consideration, the Welsh Non-Conformists were included amongst the supposed criminal; but the origin of dissension in Wales was very different from what it was in England. The Scriptures had in the days of Elizabeth had been translated into the Welsh language, but soon after, it was not, for what good reason, thought necessary to bring the Welsh over to the use, in common conversation, of the English tongue; to accomplish this, the Church service was performed everywhere in English, though not one in fifty, in most places, understood it; The Welsh complained that the Church of England, like that of Rome, withheld from the common people, the scriptures in their own language; a Welsh Bible could not be purchased; it was not in print. Itinerants, and many of them lay preachers, arose, and formed numerous congregations; they, after many difficulties, obtained an edition of the Welsh Bible. This execrable policy of attempting to force the English Language upon the Welsh, first occasioned the dissension amongst them, which, as the original cause does still, in a great measure, exist, will in all probability, end in their total defection from the Established Church. Truth itself, when heavy loaded with the armour of Hunan Policy, will sink to the ground; and the weapon, that is by absurdity, put into his hand, is the only one that can wound it

The Loyalty of the Welsh:
During the Cromwellian Civil Wars, (the same may be said of the rebellions of 1714 and 1745) no plots In Wales were formed in direct opposition to them. Yet steadfast loyalty could not screen the poor injured Welsh from the scourge of offended Priestcraft, whose infallibility they had presumed to dispute.

On the Aftermath of the Battle of St Fagan's, 1648, Cromwell's victory over Welsh forces:
There were living in Glamorgan, about thirty years ago, several old people that remembered the battle of St Fagan's; one of them assured me that the river Ely, was actually reddened by human blood; yet with all its sufferings, with all its unimpeached loyalty, so harassed were the inhabitants of Glamorgan by the scourge of Parsoncraft, that great numbers of them were obliged to fly, during the reign of Charles II, from the ruin their native country had unjustly heaped on them, to the wilds of America.

On War and Conquest
War and conquest are, generally, speaking, the aim and ambition of monarchs in all ages; to them, the slaughtering of 40 or 50,000 subjects, whose families are thereby reduced to misery and ruin, is a

thing of no moment, though this answers no other end but that of
gratifying the pride, resentment, or avarice, of a very few individuals.
It is obviously certain that Christianity, with its inseperably-attendant
Arts and Sciences, has (notwithstanding the vices that still too
much prevail) so far civilized its own part of the world, that the
arts of war are learned no more; swords have long since been beaten
into ploughshares, and spears into pruning hooks by all, except
our still unchristianized Rulers, and their minions. Were only the
governments in this respect, quiescent, it is absolutely certain that, in
no country in Europe, could any set of men, however ferocious and
unprincipled, so assemble and embody themselves together as to be
able to commit public depradations on any neighbouring people;
nor the least disposition to outrage of this nature remains amongst
those who constitute the great majority of the British nation, and
the same may be said of every other Christian nation. When Church
and State are equally civilized with those communities, over whom
they still rule with rods of iron, the Christian world will no longer
see nation rise up against nation.

On the Refinements of the Hottentots:

It does not seem to be generally known, though very true, that
Fashion derives many of its most distinguishing characteristics
from the Hottentots, a very polite people, according to modern
ideas of politeness, that inhabit the Southern parts of Africa. One
instance must suffice to present, though many more could be given;
the Hottentot, who, to use the phrase of a London oyster wench
(I should have said 'lady'!) would 'rather be out of the world than
out of the fashion,' dresses his hair with any kind of grease, and
then powders it, a la mode de Londres, with fine pulverized cow-
dung, just as in the same manner as the Cockneys use pomatum
and powder; with this difference, that the Hottentot never imports,
like Mr Reeves, any bear grease from Russia, but contents himself
with the fat of his own hog, which he thinks much better applied to
feed his poor neighbour or his chickens; he, like a good economist
makes use of the first parcel of cow fat that he finds. My Printer's
Devil, whose opinion I highly respect, assures me, that he thinks the
Hottentot by far the most rational being.

Iolo's 'Ode on Converting a Sword into a Pruning Hook':

This was recited on Primrose Hill, Hampstead, London, 'at a Meeting of Ancient British Bards resident in London, Sept 22, 1793, being the day whereon the Autumnal Equinox occurred, and one of the four grand solemn Bardic Days; under the Bardic oath, 'Gwir, yn erbyn y Byd,' 'The Truth against the World.'

Iolo quoted Isaiah 2, 4, : 'And they shall beat their swords into ploughshares, and their spears into pruning hooks; nation shall not lift up sword against nation; nor shall they learn war any more.'

A Brief Introduction to the Celtic Triads
(by Dedwydd Jones)

The Triads are poetical, ethical, historical, institutional, theological, Pauline, aphoristical, gnomic, folkloric, proverbial, often invented and practically unknown. The Poetic Triads go in threes. The Theological Triads go from divinty to infinity, also in processions of three. The whole wit and wisdom of the Celts march in columns of three. All Triads emanate from the Bards of the Isle Abounding with Beauty - Prydain. Many were re-discovered and transcribed by 1010 in manuscripts often afterwards burned, destroyed, or otherwise lost.

An Account of. and extracts from the Welsh-Bardic Triads. 'This account of the Bardic Triads was drawn up in great haste, and under anxieties that admitted of no cool attention: this was at the desire of some friends. I, too late, now observe it full of inaccuracies and blockheadisms ... I have probably mistaken the sense of some obscure passages.

The originals of these triads are in the Silurian dialect and orthography, which is the most ancient. I mention this now to obviate the carpings of those, who, properly speaking, know not this tongue.'

The Poetic Triads (or the Triads of Song)
1. The three primary requisites of poetic genius are:
An eye that can see Nature,
A heart that can feel Nature,
A resolution that dares follow Nature.

2. The Three Principal Characteristics of Poetic Genius, are:
Extraordinary understanding,
Extraordinary conduct,
Extraordinary exertion.

3. The Three Foundations of Poetic Judgment are:
Bold design,
Regular practice,

Frequent mistakes.

4. The Three things that Improve Poetic Genius, are:
Proper exertion,
Frequent exertion,
Prosperity in exertion.

5. The Three Excellencies of Poetry, are:
Complete illustration,
Profound discrimination,
Luminous composition.

6. The Three things that Improve Poetry, are:
The studying of it thoroughly,
The examining of it frequently,
The exerting of it to the utmost.

7. The Three Primary Points of Poetic Originality, are:
Where it cannot be better,
Where it cannot be otherwise,
Where there is no necessity of it being otherwise.

8. The Three Things that should be Understood in Poetry, are:
The little,
The great,
Their connectives.

9. The Three Intentions of Poetry, are:
To improve the understanding,
To cheer the heart,
To soothe the mind.

10. The Three Final Purposes of Poetry, are:
The accumulation of goodness,
The enlargement of the understanding,
The creation of delight.

11. The Three properties of a just imagination are:
What is possible,
What ought to be,
What is decorous.

12. The Three Indispensabilities of the Language of Poetry, are:
Purity,
Copiousness,
Propriety.

13. The Three Things that should be Avoided in Poetry, are:
The frivolous,
The obscure,
The superfluous.

14. The Three Principal Considerations of Poetical Description, are:
What is obvious,
What instantly engages the affections,
What is strikingly characteristic.

15. The Three Dignities of poetry, are:
The true and the wonderful united,
Beauty and sapience united,
The union of art and nature.

16. The Three Utilities of Poetry, are:
The praise of virtue and goodness,
The memory of things remarkable,
To invigorate the affections.

17. The Three Indispensable Purities of Poetry, are:
Pure truth,
Pure language,
Purity of manners.

18. Three Things should all Poetry be:
Thoroughly erudite,
Thoroughly animated,
Thoroughly natural.

19. Three Things a Bard must be most Beware of in Wales:
The horns of a bull,
The fangs of a viper,
The smile of an Englishman.

AN ACCOUN'I' OF AND EXTRACTS FROM THE WELSH BARDIC TRIADS:

'A man unacquainted with the original occasion, and, at one time, utility, of the ancient mode amongst the Welsh of writing in Triads, would pronounce it very quaint, affected, and circumscribed; cramping genius and hampering it with needless chains. Says a writer in a late periodical publication, "it is singular that the Welsh and Irish Antiquaries should continue such a lax mode of writing;" and in another place he calls the Triads "a weak production." What the Irish do, I know not, but the Welsh of the present day never write in Triads, nor have they done so these eight or ten centuries, as far as I can find, except in works of wit and humour, in the lusus scribendi: he shows but little judgment in calling it a lax mode of writing; for, too great closeness, brevity, and compression, are its greatest defects. He calls it a weak production; we will examine this a little - the first of the Triads that he was then censuring is as follows:

The Three Primary and Indispensable Requisites of Poetic Genius, are:
AN EYE THAT CAN SEE NATURE,
A HEART THAT CAN FEEL NATURE,
A RESOLUTION THAT DARES FOLLOW NATURE

This, I will venture to say, is the best, the most just and philosophical, definition of Genius that was ever given by any writer in any language; that of Dr Johnson has been said to be the best in the English language - the best extant, say some, in any tongue whatever. It is this: "True genius is a mind of large general powers, accidentally determined to some particular direction."0 Johnson, hide thy diminished head! and thou, Critical Reviewer (aut Pinkerton, aut Diabolus), in calling this a weak production, what a weak, worm-eaten figure doest thou appear! thou hast (evinced by thy rhymes and prose professed) neither Eyes that can see, nor a Heart that can feel Nature.

The Triads that are here selected are from a Manuscript

collection, by Llywelyn Sion, a Bard of Glamorgan, about the year 1560. Of this Manuscript I have a transcript; the original in the possession of Mr.Richard Bradford, of Bettws, near Bridgend, in Glamorgan. This collection was made from various manuscripts of considerable, and some of very great antiquity - these, and their authors, are mentioned, and most or all of them still extant.

The Bards and Druids (both one and the same people) of Ancient Britain, had, before letters were known, reduced the Arts of Memory and oral tradition into a well systemized science. Song was one of their methods of giving permanency or fixation to orality; songs skillfully composed on interesting subjects, were learned with avidity, they soon became popular, they could be transmitted without the aid of letters from one person, time, place, to another, though ever so remote. Long details and diffuse declamations could never be learned orally with any tolerable degree of ease, nor could they be retained in the memory; or, were it possible, and fact, in a very few extraordinary instances, it could never be so generally, or sufficiently frequent, as to be of any material use to mankind; for this reason, in addition to Song, the Bards invented a variety of aphoristical forms, on fixed, regular, and unalterable, principles, that were obvious to the understanding, easily learned and remembered, it was necessary that these should not be capable of assuming any other form, or materially different mode of verbality., than that in which they were originally delivered. Aphorisms constructed on such fixed principles could be learned with ease, and with ease be retained by the memory; they would, with nearly, if not quite as much facility as Song, become widely diffused over a large extent of Place and Time: in Songs and in Aphorisms of this description were the Theological, Ethical, and Scientifical, Maxims, of the Ancient Bards of Britain delivered, and these were easily retained by the public memory.

The term Bard, in its original Cimbric acceptation, signifies Priest; but, when letters were not known, Song having been found the best, most pleasing and for that reason the most effectual, means of fixing permanently the Oralities of Religion and useful Science, it became as indispensably necessary for a Priest to be a Poet as it is in these times for him to be able to read and write; hence Bard and Poet came in length of time to be synonymous terms.

Moderns understand nothing by the word Tradition but the wildly confused popular story of we know not what; Old wives tales; something as widely different from Bardic Tradition as the East is from the West; and, of course, whether they censure, or, in part, admit what they call tradition, they only talk nonsense, and jabber they know not what.

The Didactic Songs and Aphorisms of the Bards were always laid before their Grand Meetings, Conventions, or Curialities, of the Solstices and Equinoxes; there they were discussed with the most scrutinizing severity, if admitted at the first, they were considered at the second Meeting; and, being approved of, they were referred to the third meeting; and, being approved of by that, they were ratified or confirmed; otherwise they were referred to as the Triennial Supreme Convention for ultimate consideration, where all that had been confirmed at the Provincial Conventions were also recited, and the disciples, that there attended from every Province, enjoined to learn them, that thereby they might be as widely diffused as possible; these were recited for ever afterwards, annually at least, at every Curiality or Convention, in Britain: this being the practice, it was impossible for perversion and interpolation to take place, everything of this kind would soon be detected and rejected; all the Bardic Traditions were thus to be for ever recited annually, at one or other of the four Grand Meetings of the year: being thus guarded in every Province, it was impossible for them to deviate materially from the Truth. This well-guarded Tradition was a better Guardian of Truth than letters ever have been, especially before the art of Printing was discovered; we confide in letters that skulk in dens and dark corners; we know not whence they came into light, we often know not how they came into existence. If a manuscript has a little of the mould of age on it, we admit blindly more of what it says as truth than becomes a man. Letters can transmit lies, through a long, dark and unknown, as it were, subterraneous passage: Bardic Tradition walks in open day and beaten tracks, exposes itself to the eye of light, as its own language emphatically has it. Macpherson, Chatterton, Pinkerton, and others, could never have sported with Bardic Tradition as they have done with Letters. Nothing can more evince the fidelity of Bardic Tradition that that the Romance of Geoffrey of Monmouth is never once noticed in any Bardic Poem or Aphorism, and of each there are extant in ancient manuscripts perhaps a thousand; it is so late in the fourteenth century, and the latter end of it, before any thing of the Story of Brutus appears in the writings of any Welsh Poet, and every Poet was not a Bard. The Bards never mention, or in the least allude to, the Trojan origin of the Britons, whatever some may villainously assert. They always represent the Cymmry (Cimbri) as the Indigenes of Britain, and never give any farther account of their origin. Taliesin, by Llin Droca, (Trojan Race), means the Romans, then in this island; not the Ancient Britons.

Song, or poesy, was in the hands of Bardic Tradition, and well guarded by it from falsehood and fiction, which the Bards would by no means admit or authorize in the least; and the public would never countenance what their much-esteemed Bards rejected. It was in vain to attempt the propagation of falsehood in Verse. Long narrations and declamations in prose were unmanageable things for Tradition, they could not with ease come under its cognizance; of course it was more open than poesy to fiction; here letters were able to baffle the truth of Oral Fidelity, Art triumphed over Nature; hence it is that all the Welsh fabulous writings, as Geoffrey's History, Romances, Works of Popish superstition, etc, are in prose, nothing of the kind appears in verse till about the close of the fourteenth, or the beginning of the fifteenth centuries, when we meet with incidental mention and allusions to the Trojan fable, and the achievements of papal priestcraft. About a century before this, Edward the Bardicide, surnamed Longshanks, had caused many of the Bards to be massacred, and all were severely restricted in the exercise of their ancient functions. They were Sons of Truth and Liberty, and of course offensive to that age of tyranny and superstition; but the Welsh would not suffer them to be exterminated. Some of them continued to the time of the Reformation, and even to this day. Whatever of fable and superstition may be found in the Welsh h poetical manuscripts of the fifteenth and sixteenth centuries must not be attributed to Bardism; for, about this time, the Monks retained in their monasteries many Poets, (not Bards) that were ready and willing enough to d 0 the work of their masters; and they did it.

The Welsh Bards and their countrymen were so partial to

the science of tradition, that it was retained long after letters became generally known, it was by means of it that the Primitive Christianity of Britain came (hand in hand with Bardism) down to the present day through a long and very dark night of error and Gothic barbarity, through the flames of papal persecution; on this account the ancient Welsh Bards, though they have not yet obtained it, are as entitled to as noble a triumphal arch as that which has long ago been erected for the Waldenses. I cannot help thinking that the Patriarchs had something like the Bardic Science of Oral Tradition, and that we owe to it the accounts of the Creation, of the Deluge, the Book of Job, etc, and had we still, even in this literary age of the world, a set of men thus set apart, and supported by the community, to instruct the multitude (always very ignorant in spite of our boasted books) on the principle of Bardic Tradition, it would be in many cases useful, and no less as a counterpart to, and a watchful eye on those, that, unlooked after, commit daily the most enormous rascalities; such an institution also amongst poor unlettered Heathens would have a better and more immediate effect than a premature attempt to literate them. Why must we not indulge all the suggestions of Benevolence? why not endeavour to turn everything to the good of our poor fellow Mortals? this kind of Tradition is the most ancient, the most natural, and when duly considered, and its principles well understood, will appear evidently the most effectual method propagating Knowledge and Truth; my suggestions are highly countenanced by the example and practice of him who spake as never man did, whose Sermon on the Mount is a set of Aphorisms very much like those of the Bards of Britain, and who wrote no book, but trusted all his divine maxims to the care of Orality, where for many years they remained before they were committed to writing, and ever since we have had woeful reasons to lament that something like scientific tradition had not kept a watchful eye over the scoundrel Scribblecraft, that journeyman-thief of Priestcraft.

Of all the Aphoristical forms used by the Bards, the Triad is the most common; it is short and simple; it is constructed on fixed and unalterable principles; the relations, resemblances, and connections, of its parts to and with each other, and an object or idea wherein all are centred, render it the most useful of any.

There are some, and who can they be but academical Pedants, who strain every nerve to find something in the ancient Welsh literature to put in competition with the famed productions of Greece and Rome; they will not be successful in this, excepting some of our ancient Odes and Pastorals. These men, seeking for what cannot be found, neglect as unworthy of their notice, what we have of Ancient Wisdom so originally and very singularly our own, that there is no place where it could possibly be borrowed from. Our Ethics have a beautiful sublimity, our Poetical criticism is equal to that of any language, our system of versification is superior to any thing of its kind, perhaps, in the World, is reduced to twenty-four elementary classes, and there is not any language, ancient or modern, any kind of verse to be found that is not used in the Welsh language, and that does not rank under one or the other of our twenty-four primary classes all the principles, all the varieties, all the combinations, of verse that exist in nature, belong to one or other of these, and we have in common use many kinds so singularly different from what has ever yet been known in any part of ancient or modern Europe, that no conception of them can well be conveyed to one unacquainted with the Welsh language; and amongst these are some of the most harmonious that any language can be susceptible of. This system of versification is no modern thing; for, we have it in manuscripts of 500 years standing; it was completed, and received in its highest and ultimate polish, when every other European language, now living, was yet in the dark womb of barbarity.

After what I have said of the origin and occasion of the Triads, the candid reader will rather attend to the nature of the sentiment than to the cramped mode of expressing it, and judge of their author's abilities, by what, with such ideas, he would have performed in the modern modes of literature, rather than what he was necessitated to do we know not how many centuries ago, when written dissertations were not known, and could be of no use.

The Triads are titled in Welsh, 'Trioedd Beirdd Ynys Prydain,' that is, 'The Triads of the Bards of the Island of Britain:' They are classed under various heads, of Institutes, Ethics, Poetical Criticism, etc, and of each I will give a specimen, as I already have of the poetic Triads.

THE INSTITUTIONAL TRIADS

1. The First Three Institutional Bards of Britain, were
Plennydd,
Alawn,
Gwron.

2. For Three Reasons why the Bards are titled 'Bards', according to the rights and institutes of the Bards of the Island of Britain:
First, because Bardism originated in Britain;
Second, because pure Bardism was never well understood in any other country;
Third, because pure Bardism can never be preserved and continued but by means of the Institutes and Voice-conventional of the Bards of the Island of Britain; for this reason, of whatever country they might be, they are titled Bards, according to the rights and Institutes of the Bards of the Island of Britain.

3. The Three Memorials of the Bards of the Island of Britain, are:
The Memorial of Song,
The Memorial of Bardic Voice-conventional,
The Memorial of ostensible Usage.

4. Of Three Descriptions are the Bards of the Island of Britain:
Primitive Bards (instituted before Christianity),
The Bards of Beli (since Christianity),
The Bards Dissentient.

5. There are Three Orders of the Primitive Bards:
The Ruling Bard, or Primitive Bard positive, according to the rights, voice, and usage, of the Bardic Conventions, whose office it is to superintend and regulate;
The Ovate (or Euvate), according to genius, exertion, and incident; whose avocation it is to act on the principles of inventive genius;
The Druid, according to reason, nature, and necessities, of things; and his office is to instruct.

6. The Three Primary Privileges of the Bards of the Island of Britain, are:
Maintenance wherever they go,
No naked weapon be borne in their presence,
Their testimony preferred to that of all others.

7. The Three Ultimate Intentions of Bardism, are:
To reform morals and customs,
To secure peace,
To celebrate the praises of all that is good and excellent.

8. Three Things are Forbidden to a Bard:
Immorality,
Mockery,
Bearing arms.

9. The Three Modes of Instruction used by the Bards of the Island of Britain:
The dictates of the Voice-conventional,
Of song,
Of usage conventional.

10. The Three Joys of the Bards of the Island of Britain:
The Increase of knowledge,
The reformation of manners,
The triumph of peace over the lawless and depredatory.

11. The Three Splendid Triumphs of the Bards of the Island of Britain:
The triumph of learning over ignorance,
The triumph of reason over irrationality,
The triumph of peace over the lawless and depredatory.

12. The Three Congenialities (or attributes) of the Bards of the Island of Britain:
To make truth manifest and diffuse the knowledge of it,

To perpetuate the praise of all that is good and excellent,
With peace to prevail over the lawless and depredatory.

13. The Three Necessary, but Reluctant, Duties of the Bards of the Island of
Britain:
Secrecy for the sake of peace and the public good,
Invective lamentation required by justice,
To unsheathe the sword against the lawless and depredatory.

14. Three Things that cannot be Contraverted:
The usages,
The song,
The voice of Bardic convention.

15. Three Things must be Preserved by the Bards:
The Cimbric language,
Primitive Bardism,
The remembrance of all that is good and excellent.

16. Without these Three Qualifications no one can be a Bard:
Poetical genius,
The knowledge of the Bardic institutes,
Irreproachable morals.

17. There are Three Avoidant Injunctions on the Bard:
To avoid sloth as being the man of diligence and exertion,
To avoid contention as being the man of peace,
To avoid folly as being the man of reason.

18. Three Nations Corrupted what was Taught them of British Bardism,
Blending with it heterogeneal principles, by which means they lost it:
The Scots (Irish),
The Latavian Cimbri (The Bretons of France),
The Germans.

These contain most of the leading maxims of the British Bardic Institutions: how they may illustrate, correct, and be corrected by, what the Greek and Roman writers have related of the Bards and Druids, let the learned enquire. Of all the modern Bardic historians, not one has given us a single word of truth, or anything like good sense, but Mr W. Owen, prefixed to his lately published translation from the Welsh of the Poetical Works of Llywarch Hen.'

THE THEOLOGICAL TRIADS

1. There are Three Primeval Unities, and more than one of each cannot exist:
One God,
One Truth,
One point of Liberty (and this is where all opposites equiponderate.)

2. Three Things Proceed from the Three Primeval Unities:
All of Life,
All that is Good,
All Power.

3. God Consists Necessarily of Three Things:
The greatest of Life,
The greatest of Knowledge,
The greatest of Power (and of what is the greatest there can be no more than one of any thing.)

4. Three Things it is Impossible God should not be:
Whatever perfect Goodness should be,
Whatever perfect Goodness would desire to be,
Whatever perfect Goodness can perform.

5. Three Things Evince what God has done and will do:
Infinite Power,
Infinite Wisdom,
Infinite Love,
For there is nothing that these attributes want of Power, of Knowledge, or of Will, to perform.

6. The Three Regulations of God towards Giving Existence to Every Thing:
To annihilate the power of evil,
To assist all that is good,

To make discrimination manifest (that it might be known what should and should not be.)

7. Three Things it is Impossible that God should not Perform:
What is most beneficial,
What all want most,
What is most beautiful of all things.

8. The Three Stabilities of Existence:
What cannot be otherwise,
What need not be otherwise,
What cannot be conceived better.
(And in these will all things end.)

9. Three Things will Infallibly be Done:
All that is possible for the Power,
All that is possible for the Wisdom,
All that is possible for the Love of God to perform.

10. The Three Grand Attributes of God:
The Infinite Plenitude of Life,
The Infinite Plenitude of Knowledge,
The Infinite Plenitude of Power.

11. There are Three Circles (or States) of Existence:
The Circle of Infinity, (where there is nothing but God,
of the living or dead, (and none but God can traverse them.)
The Circle of Inchoation, (where all things are by Nature derived
from Death. This Circle has been traversed by Man.)
The Circle of Felicity, (where all things spring from Life; this circle
Man shall traverse in Heaven.)

13. Animated Beings have Three States of Existence:
Inchoation in the Great Deep (or Lowest point of existence)
Liberty in the state of Humanity,
Love, which is Felicity, in Heaven.

14. All Animated Beings are Subject to Three Necessities:
A beginning in the Great Deep (or lowest point of existence),
Progression in the Circle of Inchoation,
Plenitude in Heaven, or the Circle of Felicity,
(Without these things nothing can possibly exist but GOD.)

15. Three Things are Necessary in the Circle of Inchoation:
The least of all animation (and thence the beginning),
The materials of all things (and thence increase, which cannot take place in any other state),
The Formation of things out of the dead mass (hence, discriminate individuality.)

16. Three Things cannot but Exist towards all Animated Beings from the Nature of Divine Justice:
Co-sufferance in the Circle of Inchoation, (because without that none could attain the perfect knowledge of any thing)
Co-participation in the Divine Love,
Co-ultimity from the Nature of God's Power, and its attributes of Justice and Mercy.

17. There are Three Necessary Occasions of Inchoation (metempsychosis) to collect the materials and properties of every Nature:
To collect the knowledge of every thing,
To collect Power towards subduing the Adverse and Devastative,
And for the devastation of Evil;
(Without this traversing of every mode of animated existence, no state of animation, or of any thing in Nature, can attain to Plenitude)

18. The Three Great, or Primary, Infelicities of the Circle of Inchoation:
Necessity,
Loss of memory,
Death.

19. There are Three Principal Indispensabilities (necessities) before Plenitude of Knowledge can be obtained:
To traverse the Circle of Inchoation,
To traverse the Circle of Felicity,
To recover the memory of all things, down to the Great Deep.

20. Three Things are Indispensably Connected with the State of Inchoation:
No subjection to injunctive laws (because it is impossible for any actions to
be there otherwise than they are,)
The Escape of Death from all Evil and Devastation,
The Accumulation of Life and Good,
(by becoming divested of Evil in the Escapes of Death; and all through Divine Love embracing all things.)

21. The Three Instrumentalities of God in the Circle of Inchoation, towards subduing Evil and Devastation:
Necessity,
Loss of Memory,
Death.

22. There are three Connates:
Man,
Liberty,
Light.

23. The Three Necessary Incidents of Humanity:
To suffer,
To change,
To choose,
(and man, having the power of choosing, it is impossible before occurrence to foresee what his sufferings and changes will be.)

24. The Three Equiportions of Humanity:
Inchoation and Felicity,
Necessity and Liberty,

Evil and Good,
(Man having the power of attaching himself to either the one or the other.)

25. From Three Causes will the Necessity of Re-inchoation Fall on Man:

From not endeavouring to obtain knowledge,
From non-attachment to Good,
Attachment to Evil,
(Occasioned by these things he will fall down to his co-natural state in the Circle of Inchoation, whence, at first, he returns to Humanity.)

26. For Three Reasons must Man unavoidably Fall into the Circle of Inchoation, though he has in Every thing else Attached himself to Good:

Pride, for which he falls down to the utmost of the Great Deep, or lowest point of existence,
 Falsehood (untruth), to a state corresponding to his turpitude,
Cruelty into a corresponding state of brutal malignity, whence, as at first, he returns to the state of Humanity.

27. Three Things are Primitial in the State of Humanity:

The accumulation of Knowledge,
The blessings of Benevolence,
Power, without undergoing Dissolution (Death.)
These are called the Three Victories, and cannot be done, as of Liberty and Choice, in any state previous to Humanity.

28. The Three Victories over Evil and Devastation, are:

Knowledge,
Love (Benevolence),
Power,
(for these know how, have the will, and the Power, in their conjunctive capacities, to effect all they can desire; these begin, and are for ever continued, in the state of Humanity.)

29. The Three Privileges of the State of Humanity:
Equiponderance of Good and Evil, (whence comparitivity),
Liberty of Choice, (whence judgment and preference),
The origin of Power, (proceeding from Judgment and Preference),
These being indispensably prior to all other exertions.

30. In Three Things Man unavoidably Differs from God:
Man is finite,
God is infinite,
Man had a beginning, which God could not have,
Man not being able to endure Eternity, must have in the Circle of Felicity a rotatory change of his mode of existence; God is under no such necessity, being able to endure all things, and that consistent with Felicity.

31. Three Things are Primitial in the Circle of Felicity:
The Cessation of Evil,
The Cessation of Want,
The Cessation of Perishing.

32. The Three Restorations of the Circle of Felicity:
Restoration of Original Genius and character,
Restoration of all that was primaevally beloved,
Restoration of Remembrance from the origin of all things, (without these, perfect Felicity cannot subsist.)

33. Three Things Discriminate every Animated Being from All Others:
Original genius,
Peculiarity of Remembrance,
Peculiarity of Perception,
 (each of these in its Plenitude, and two Plenitudes of any thing cannot exist.)

34. With Three Things has God Endued every Animated Being:
With all the Plenitude of his own Nature,
With Individuality differing from that of all others,

With an original and peculiar Character and Genius, which is that of no other being, hence in every being a Plenitude of that Self, differing from all others.   .

35. By the Knowledge of Three Things will all Evil and Death be Diminished and subdued:

Their Nature,

Their Cause,

Their Operations,

(this knowledge will be obtained in the Circle of Felicity.)

36. The Three Stabilities of Knowledge, are:

To have traversed every state of animated existence,

To remember every state and its incidents,

To be able to traverse all states of animation that can be desired, for the sake of experience and judgment, (this will be obtained in the Circle of Felicity.)

37. The Three Peculiar Distinctions of every Being in the Circle of Felicity are:

Vocation,

Privilege,

Character (Disposition),

(Nor is it possible for any two beings to be uniformly the same in every thing, for, everyone will possess Plenitude, of what constitutes his incommunicable distinction from all others; and there can be no plenitude of any thing without having it in a degree that comprehends the whole of it that can exist.)

38. Three Things None but God can Do:

Endure the Eternities of the Circle of Infinity,

Participate of every state of existence without changing,

To reform and renovate everything without causing the loss of it.

39. Three Things can never be Annihilated, from their Unavoidable possibilities:

Mode of existence,

Essentials of existence,

The Unity of every mode of existence,

(These will, divested of their Evils, exist for ever, as the varieties of the Good and Beautiful in the Circle of Felicity.)

40. The Three Excellencies of Changing Modes of Existence in the Circle of Felicity:

Acquisition of Knowledge,

Beautiful variety,

Repose from not being able to endure uniform Infinity and uninterrupted Eternity.

41. Three Things Increase Continually:

Fire, or Light,

Understanding, or Truth,

Soul, or Life,

(these will prevail over everything else, and then the state of Inchoation will cease.)

42. Three Things Dwindle away Continually:

The Dark,

The False,

The Dead.

43. Three Things Accumulate strength Continually, there being a Majority of Desires towards them:

Love,

Knowledge,

Justice.

44. Three Things Become more and more Enfeebled Daily, there being a Majority of Desires in opposition to them:

Hatred,

Injustice,

Ignorance.

45. The Three Plenitudes of Felicity:

Participation of every nature with a plenitude of One predominant, Conformity to every call of Genius and Character, possessing superior excellence in One,
The love of all beings and existences, but chiefly centred on one object, which is God; and in the Predominant One of each of these will the Plenitude of Felicity consist.

46. The Three Necessary Essentials of God:
Infinite in himself,
Finite to finite comprehensions,
Co-unity with every mode of existence in the Circle of Felicity.

These Triads have often a air of tautology, occasioned by this very circumscribed mode of dictating in short aphorisms that afford not room for sufficient explication, whence the necessity of resuming a subject in a second, third, or fourth, Triad; and perhaps, oftener on some occasions.

I find but very little assistance from the technology of Modern (derived from the Grecian) Metaphysics, in my attempts to render the language of Bardism into English, and have made no great use of it.

THE ETHICAL TRIADS

The Bardic Theology, and the morality deduced from it, are truly Patriarchical, pure, and sublime. I shall here insert a few Ethical Triads, or, as they are titled, Triads of Wisdom.

1. The Three Primary Principles of Wisdom:
Obedience to the Laws of GOD,
Concern for the Welfare of Mankind,
Suffering with Fortitude all the accidents of life.

2. The Three Great Laws of Man's Actions:
What he forbids in another,
What he requires from another,
What he cares not how it is done by another.

3. Three Things Well understood will give Peace:
The tendencies of Nature,
The Claims of Justice,
The Voice of Truth.

4. There are Three ways of Searching the Heart of Man:
In the thing he is not aware of,
In the manner he is not aware of,
At the time he is not aware of.

5. There are Three Things, and God will not love him that loves to look at them:
Fighting,
A Monster,
The pomposity of Pride.

6. Three Things Produce Wisdom:
Truth,
Consideration,
Suffering.

7. The Three Great Ends of Knowledge:
Duty,
Utility,
Decorum.

8. There are Three Men that all ought to look upon with Affection:
He that, with affection, looks upon the face of the earth,
He that is delighted with rational works of art,
He that looks lovingly on little infants.

9. Three Men will not Love their Country:
He that loves luxurious food,
He that loves riches,
He that loves ease.

10. Three Things may be Observed in a Woman,
(and loving the first, she will not dislike the other two) :
Her own face in the mirror,
Her husband's back afar off,
A gallant in her bed.

11. The Three Laughs of a fool:
At the Good,
At the Bad,
At he knows not what.

12. Three Things Corrupt the World:
Pride,
Superfluity,
Indolence.

THE TRIADS OF ST PAUL:
We have a set of Triads entitled 'Trioedd Pawl' (Paul's triads). They are a selection of the Christian doctrines put into this aphoristical form, and thus adapted to Bardic recitation and tradition.

1. There are three Sorts of Men:
The man of God, who renders Good for Evil,
The Man of Man, who renders Good for Good, and Evil for Evil,
The Man of the Devil, who renders evil for Good.

2. Three Sorts of People are the Delight of God:
The Meek,
Lovers of Peace,
Lovers of mercy.

3. There are Three Marks of the Children of God:
A humble demeanour,
A pure Conscience,
The suffering of injuries patiently.

4. The Three Principal Things Required by God:
Love,
Justice,
Humility.

5. In Three Places will be Found the Most of God:
Where he is mostly sought,
Where he is mostly loved,
Where there is the least of self.

6. There are Three sorts of Lies:
Verbal lies,
The lies of silence,
The lies of false appearance,
(each inducing us to believe what we should noi.)

7. Three Things shall a Man Obtain by a Belief in God:
What is necessary in this life,
A peaceable Conscience,
Communion with Heaven.

8. The Three Counsels given by Lazarus:
'Believe in God, who made thee!
Love God, who redeemed thee,
Fear God, who will judge thee!'

9. Three Ways a Christian Punishes an Enemy:
By forgiving him,
By not divulging his wickedness,
By doing him all the good that is possible.

10. The Three Concerns of a Christian:
Lest he should offend God,
Lest he should be a stumbling block to Man,
Lest his love for all that is Good should fail.

11. The Three Evidences of Holiness:
Self-denial,
A liberal disposition,
The encouragement of all that is Good.

12. Three Three Dainties of Christian Festivity, are:
What God has prepared,
What can be obtained consistent with justice,
What love to all can venture to use.

13. Three Persons have the Claims and Privileges of Brothers and Sisters:
Orphans,
Widows,
Aliens.

These were the doctrines inculcated by the Welsh Bards in those

Dark Ages, when Rome preached up what was very different.

Other Triads:

There are further Triads - on Reincarnation and Immateriality, Modes of Existence, the Voice Conventionals, and the astonishing Curialities! The history of the Isle Abounding with Beauty is given too, all in triadic incantations, as with these:

The Three Grave-slaughtering ones,
The Three Men of Illusion and Fantasy,
The Three Niggardly Stocks,
The Three Immense Feasts,
The Three Perpetual Harmonies,
The Three Princely Varieties,
The Three Frivolous Bards,
The Three Fettered Men,
The Three Red Ravishers,
The Three Slaughter Blocks,
The Three Powerful Swineherds,
The Three Great Enchantments,
The Three Savage Men who performed the Three Unfortunate Assassinations,
The Three Disclosures
The Three Great Concealments,
The Three Faithless Wives,
The Three Prominent Cows, and, yes,
The Three Well-endowed Men!
The Three Men who Received the Wisdom of Adam,
The Three Women who Received the Beauty of Eve.
The Three Golden Corpses,
The Three Bull Spectres,
The Three Great defilements,
The Three Joyless Wonderers.

Most impressive of all, perhaps, are the Nine Impulsive Stocks of the Baptismal Bards of the Isle Abounding with Beauty, while the most melancholy must be The Three who Broke their Hearts from

Bewilderment.

A Word on Faith:
'But how much of all this can you really believe?'
'Believe everything and believe nothing.'
'Why?'
'Because little is known of the Great Bidder or Mysterious Thing of the World.'
'Why 'Bards' at all?'
'To make conspicuous.'
'To make what conspicuous?'
'The Truth.'
'What?'
'The Truth - against the world.'
'How?'
'In the eye of light, in the face of the sun,'
'But where?'
'Begin with the Triads of the Isle Abounding with Beauty. That is all.'

An Account of the Proceedings at the Carmarthen Eisteddfod, 1819, by Jonathan Harris, Printer and Publisher, in his introduction to his 'Two Prize Essays, at the Eisteddfod.

'The Mother of Poets and Poetry - the 'proceedings of the Eisteddfod, or Congress of Bards,' held at Carmarthen on Thursday 8th of July, 1819,' proclaiming the 'Distinctive and Comprehensive advantages of the Bardic Institutions of Carmarthen and Glamorgan, was 'dedicated to the President of the Eisteddfod, the Lord Bishop of St David's, a zealous advocate and successful asserter of the right of the Welsh nation to retain and cultivate its ancient tongue.'

'At the 1819 Carmarthen Eisteddfod, Edward Williams, Iolo Morganwg, officially established for the first time, the ceremonies initiated on Primrose Hill, Hampstead, London. Iolo was selected as Officiating Bard, and conferred on eight chosen Bards, the much sought after 'B.B.D.' ('Bardd Braint a Defod - Bard by Privilege and Custom.')
    Iolo 'commenced the ceremony by making out a circle with small stones, placing a large one in the centre, and none but admitted bards would presume to enter the circle. Iolo took a sheathed sword from the Sword Bearer, and this was unsheathed by the several bards standing within the circle, each one of them at the same time laying a hand on the hilt of the sword and the Officiating Bard holding the point of the scabbard. The latter proceeded to indicate the qualities expected in a candidate for the degree of Bard, emphasizing that it would not be possible to admit anyone other than on the recommendations of a Bard who was present, or by examination of his skill in Poetic Composition. The ceremony of admission, after suitable commendation and unanimous approval, was performed by the Officiating Bard, who held the sword with its point towards him, while the entrant held the hilt, the former observing to the latter, that, once admitted, he would be under obligation not to show violence towards any man with the sword. After receiving him, the

Officiating Bard tied a blue ribbon about his right arm. When all the Bards had been admitted, the sword was place upon the stone at the centre of the circle.

While candidates were being admitted to the Degree of Druid, the sword rested upon the stone at the centre of the circle and after due praise of the candidate had been received, and his qualifications recited, with no one dissenting, he was received by the Officiating Bard, who tied a white ribbon about his right arm. The admission of others to the degree of Ovates was similarly carried out, except that these were adorned with green ribbons. After all the candidates had been admitted, the sword was taken up and all the bards touched its hilt as the Officiating Bard held the sheath into which the sword had been driven; and with this, the ceremony ended. The blue ribbon worn by the Bards, is a symbol of Truth; the white, of innocence; the green, of the arts.'

The concluding Address of Iolo Morganwg:

The concluding address of Edward Williams (Iolo Morganwg) Romancer, Remembrancer, Embellisher, Regulator, Reformer, Polisher of the Tribe, that is 'Prydydd' – poet! at the Carmarthen Eisteddfod 1819. His researches into Welsh lore, both real and fabulous, formed the basis of the 1819 Congress of Bards, and all subsequent eisteddfodau, up to the present day. Iolo's tremendous, patriotic, unifying vision of Wales still draws all Welsh folk together.

Iolo:

'This Eisteddfod commenced on Thursday, the 8th of July, between the hours of eleven and twelve in the forenoon, in the great room of the Ivy Bush Hotel, with the sound of trumpets; when a great concourse of persons, consisting of Members of the Cambrian Society, Bards, and Musicians, assembled at a given signal, all of whom were admitted by tickets, on which their names were written, none besides having the privilege of being present. His Lordship, Lord Dynevor, whose ancestor Gruffydd ap Nicholas, that respected nobleman and illustrious patron of the Bards, was represented by The Right Reverend Dr Burgess, Lord Bishop of St David's whose zeal and well-directed exertions on the occasion, were equally conspicuous and successful.

At the opening of the Proceedings, Mr Edward Williams, the old bard of Glamorganshire, appeared, leaning on the arm of the young Bard of Cardiganshire; and the contrast between youth and age - the aspirant and the proficient, rendered the circumstance peculiarly interesting. The Bardic chair, or chair of merit, constructed for the occasion of indigenous oak, in the pure Gothic style, was placed on a table, in order to gratify the curiosity of the company, as well as to excite the emulation of those who might feel desirous of occupying it. The Eisteddfod was opened by the officiating President, surrounded by the Committee of Management, the judges appointed for rewarding the prizes for the best literary compositions, and several Bards and Musicians, amounting with others to about two hundred persons, were present. The business of the meeting was opened by the learned and worthy Prelate who filled the chair, in a short but highly appropriate speech. This speech which was received with long-continued plaudits being ended,

Mr Edward Williams rose, and addressed the Meeting as follows:

'To what his Lordship has so elegantly and so pointedly to the purpose said, I can add but little! I can add but little; yet I humbly beg leave to make a few observations. One of the principal objects of the Cambrian Literary Society, is the cultivation of our national poetry, and the restoration of it to its ancient character - that of being the guardian and teacher of truth. Poetry has in the infancy of all nations hitherto known to us, been the primeval vehicle of knowledge; it has been the incipiency of literature. At an early period of the world, the CYMMRY (Kimmeri) became civilized by the moral and sentimental songs of their primitive Bards, to a considerable degree, 'in the light of the song,' they became united in a social compact. The remains of their ancient Bardic and druidical learning are to this day amongst us, and exhibit such high attainments of genuine wisdom, as . cannot be generally found amongst the nations of this world. Poetry had preserved to us our original language to this day, in all its pristine purity, through very dark periods of ignorance, wherein all the languages of the numerous nations of the vast Roman Empire expired; the noble Greek language, which had subsisted 2,000 years in almost unaltered purity, has become-extinct; the Latin, the language legally established of this enormous empire, has been for more than a thousand years, a dead language; the Ancient British Language is still alive - in it are authentic specimens of literature, which are to this day easily understood. The language of Wales is the only language that has survived the death of the Empire of Rome, and all its other languages. The cultivation of the literature of this language has excited the energetic attention of the Right Rev. founder and father of the highly respectable Cambrian Literary Society, which exhibits itself before us this day; a day which we announce as the resurrection day of learning in our greatly beloved native language; this day dawns in high splendour at Carmarthen. Carmarthen had, nearly four hundred years ago, the highly-merited honour of appearing a bright star in the dawn of a stormy day; short indeed and wintery was the day which ensued; and fraught with the storms which issued, as it were, from their dens, in the house of York and Lancaster; those storms have, we thank the adorable Divine Providence, long since expended their last breath. We live in halcyon days of peace; let us hope that, by future ages, they may be recorded as days of pure religion and morality; and let us, who live in these days, endeavour to establish their character as such. In the year 1451, a Grand Eisteddfod was held at Carmarthen, under the auspices of that truly great man, Gruffydd ap Nicholas: his noble descendent and lover of his country, appears as the coadjutor of our most worthy Bishop of St David's; his hand energetically assists in laying the foundation stone of our splendid institution; and, under this noble patronage, we this day behold and rejoice in another grand literary festival at Carmarthen. From Carmarthen, as from a central point, may the angels of knowledge, of learning, of all virtues of which the human mind may be susceptible, take their flights in every direction, on the wings of all the winds, showering from their golden pinions upon us the intellectual blessings of pure wisdom, peace, and happiness. Where is the man, who, wishing to be considered as a lover of his country, that would not wish, and to the utmost exert himself, to secure success to this grandly benign intention?"

'This speech elicited unbounded applause.'

Jonathan Harris finishes:
'At the conclusion, it was proposed, that the thanks of the Meeting be given to the Lord Bishop of St David's, the officiating President, for the great pains he had taken in promoting the interests of Cambria, and the ability with which his Lordship had executed the duties of his office during the whole of the Eisteddfod, which motion was received and passed with acclamation, and the Meeting was declared to be closed. The company appeared to be highly gratified with the various proceedings they had witnessed; and to depart under a deep impression of the beneficial tendency of the Institution.'

'Mr Edward Williams (Iolo) and Mr Robert Davies, had five guineas each, towards defraying their expenses.'

Inscribed on Iolo's Bardic Chair, or Chair of Merit, Carmarthen, 1819:
'Gwir yb erbyn y Byd' (Truth against the World)
Canol wrth Galon. (Heart to heart).

Regalia and Costumes: Circa 1880

'Sir Hubert Herkomer, RA, the son of a Bavarian wood-carver, designed the eisteddfodic robes, keeping in mind Iolo's injunction that they should be of a uniform and symbolic colour. Hence, the robe of the order of Ovates is green, to signify the Novitiate's growth and increase in learning and science. The order of Bards, Musicians and Literati wear a blue robe to signify the sky-blue colour perceptible in serene summer weather, as an indication of peace and tranquillity and that all visible things are seen best in that heavenly light. The Druidic Order's robes is white 'in token of that uncompromising and unsullied Truth which should claim their full allegiance whether in Art or Science, in accordance with the motto of that Order, The Truth against the World.'

The Sword of Peace:

The Grand Sword of Peace was also designed by Herkomer. 'The natural crystal in the hilt stands for mystery. Within it are drilled the three sacred lines supposed to be the first attempt to write to Jehovah, the dragon guarding both. The hand-guard is of wrought steel, the dragon and handle of copper gilt. The scabbard being of wood, symbolizes peace. On the five bands that encircle the scabbard will be found embossed the words, 'Y gwir yn erbyn y byd, Duw a phob daioni, Calon wrth galon, A laddo a leddir, Iesu na ad gamwaith.' (Truth against the World, God and all goodness, Heart to Heart. He who kills shall be killed! Jesus, let no oppression persist!' 'The mottoes of the provinces of Wales: Morganwg, Gwent, Powys, Dyfed,. Gwynedd.'

The Crown.

'I saw the crown of the Archdruid of oak-leaves and acorns being made, with a spray of oak beside it, from which it was copied in metal, and a copy of an ancient British breastplate and a crystal-headed sceptre to go with it.'

The Banner

'The Banner was designed by the Herald Bard, and comprised a sky-blue background embroidered in gold with oak leaves, leeks and mistletoe. On its upper part is a rampant dragon in the centre of a radiant sun, three rays of which form the mystic sign, and between the rays are woven the Gorsedd mottoes: Yng ngwyneb haul llygad goleuni (In the face of the sun, in the eye of light), and Y Gwir yn erbyn y byd (Truth against the World.). In the lower half is a circle of crystals, representing the Gorsedd (throne) Circle, in which is inscribed the word 'Heddwch.' (Peace.)'

The Eisteddfod Today and Tomorrow.

The national Eisteddfod cannot be held unless it is proclaimed a year and a day in advance. The proclamation must take place within the Gorsdedd Circle. The Circle consists of 12 pillars hewn from local stone, with a flat-topped stone, the Logan Stone, at the centre, which provides a platform for the Archdruid to conduct the ceremonies. Facing the Logan Stone, at the east cardinal point, is the Stone of the Covenant, where the Herald Bard stands. Behind this are the Portal Stones, which are guarded by purple-robed eisteddfod officials. The Portal Stone to the right points to the sunrise on midsummer day, the stone to the left indicates the rising sun during mid-winter. The shadows cast by these three stones form the pattern /1\, symbolising Love, Justice, and Truth. This mystic mark is known as the Mark of the Shafts of Light. The ceremony opens with a fanfare of trumpets from banner-bearers in crimson tunics. This is followed by the eisteddfod prayer:

Grant, 0 God, Thy protection,
And in protection, strength,
And in strength, understanding,
And in understanding, perception of righteousness,
And in the perception of righteousness, the love of it,
And in the love of it, the love of all life,
And in all life, to love God,
　God and all goodness.

With his regalia of bronze and gold, the Archdruid ascends the Logan stone. He performs the opening ceremony by laying his hand on the partially drawn blade of the Grand Sword and, calling out to the assembly, 'Is there peace?' He repeats this call three times, sheathing the sword after each massed response of 'There is peace!' The Archdruid then accepts the Hirlas Horn (of Plenty), symbolizing the welcome of the neighbourhood in which the eisteddfod is being held. He then receives a bouquet of wild flowers from a troop of young girls, who then perform a floral dance. The dance is also performed during the chairing and crowning of the Bard ceremonies.

The dancers wear cloaks of vermilion traced with gold, over white silk gowns, and a flowering headdress of gold-lame, with chaplets and garlands of wild flowers.' .

The Climactic:
'The culminating point of the Congress, is the Crowning of the Bard. This ceremony is conducted 'according to the rites of the Bards of the Isle of Britain,' and is 'under the direction of the Gorsedd of Bards. The winning Bard will be proclaimed by the sound of trumpets; the Gorsedd Recorder will call the Muster of Bards; the Adjudication will be delivered; the winning Bard, unknown up to that moment, will be escorted to the platform by two of the Principal Bards and invested as Crowned Bard of the eisteddfod for that year. The Bards will then deliver their addresses, and the Crowning Song will be sung.'

The Three Finest Fables of the Isle Abounding with Beauty, are:
The Fable born on Primrose Hill, 1792,
The Fable perpetuated at the Carmarthen Eisteddfod, 1819
The Fable which has flourished every year ever since.

'Love thy nation; remember the Past!'
Gwalchmai the Golden Tongued (circa 6th century)

www.ingramcontent.com/pod-product-compliance
Lightning Source LLC
Chambersburg PA
CBHW022125170526
45157CB00004B/1756